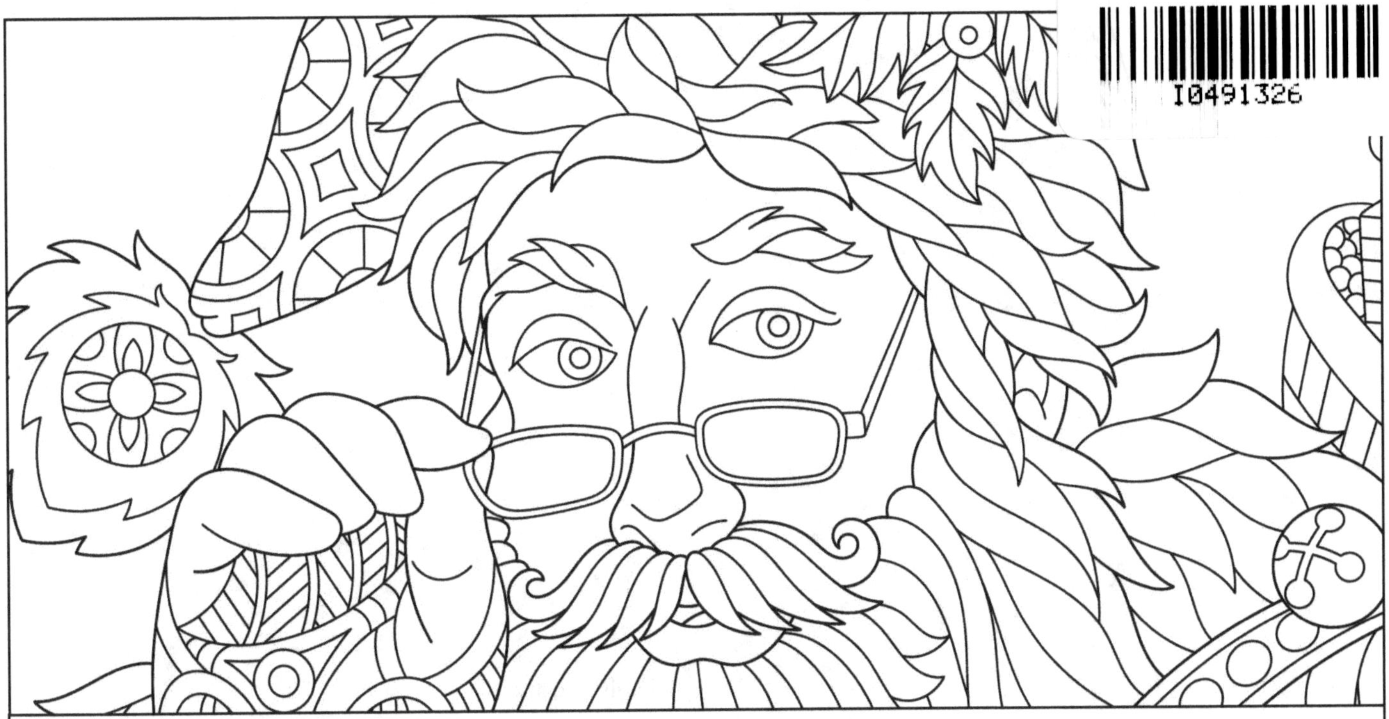

simply creative

CHRISTMAS

coloring book for adults

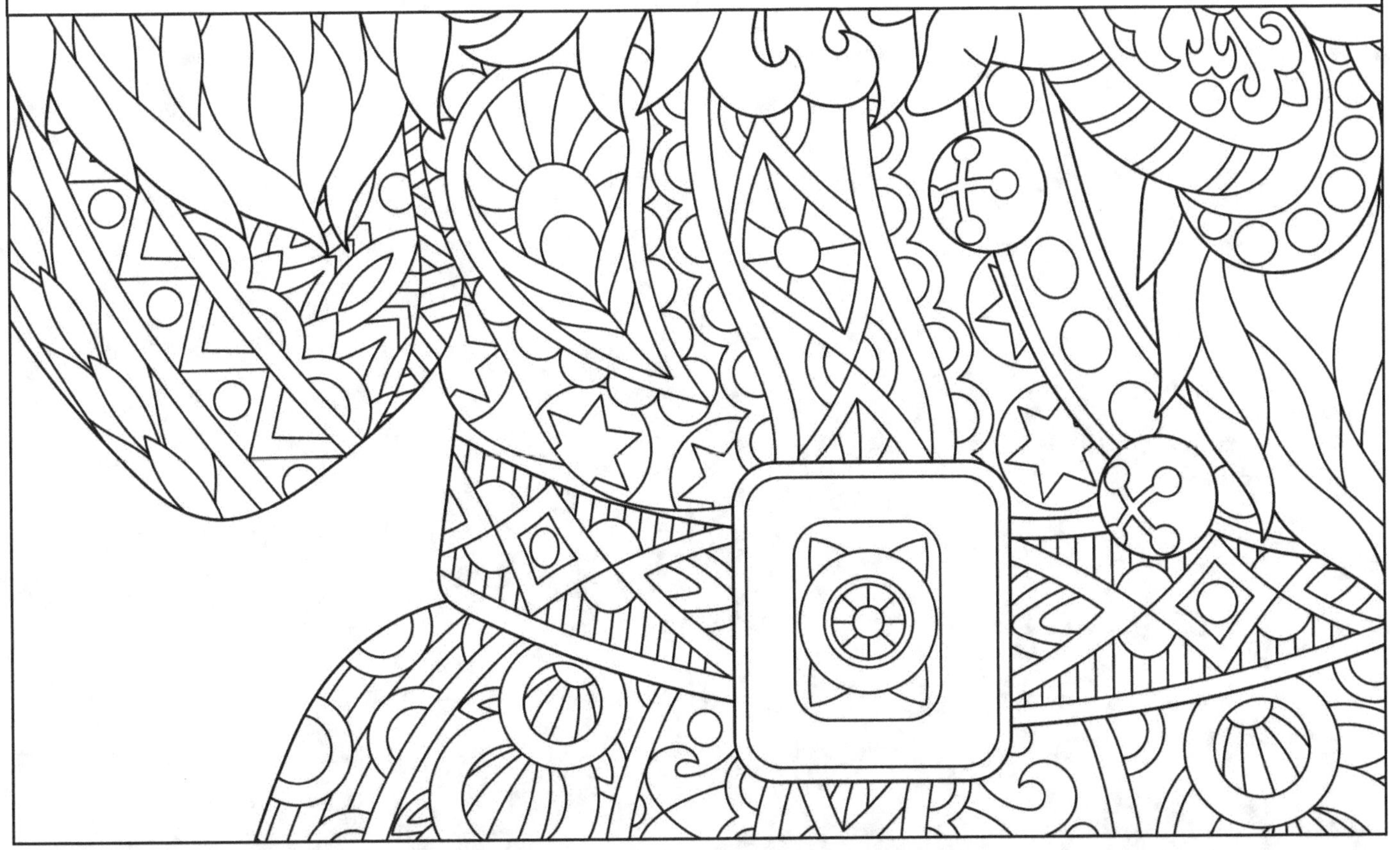

Design by Lynne Dempsey
Art courtesy of Creative Market, 123RF, Storyblocks, and The Hungry JPEG.

Printed in the United States of America
First Printing 2017
ISBN 978-1-944474-17-1

www.simplycreativepublishing.com

This book belongs to:

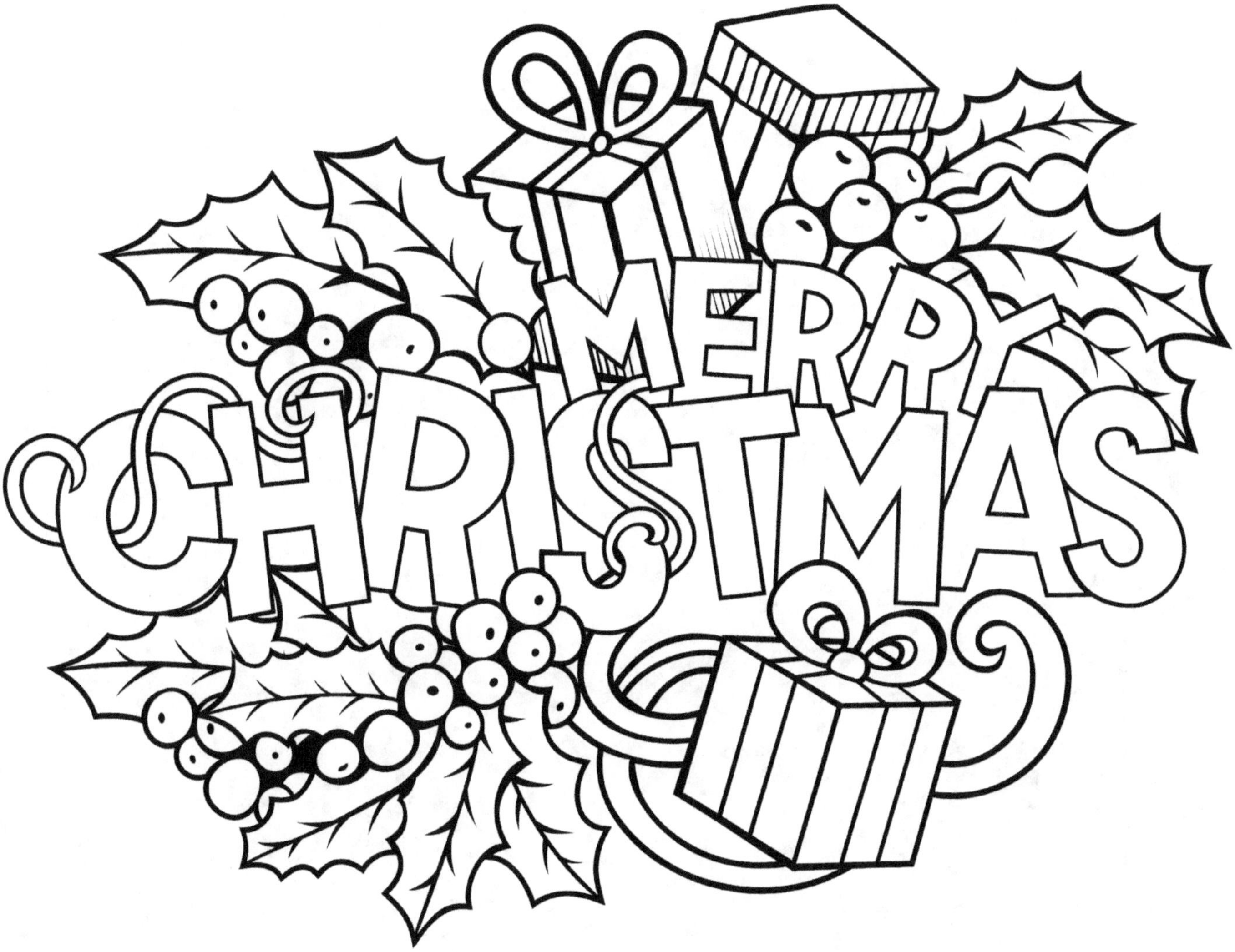
MERRY
CHRISTMAS

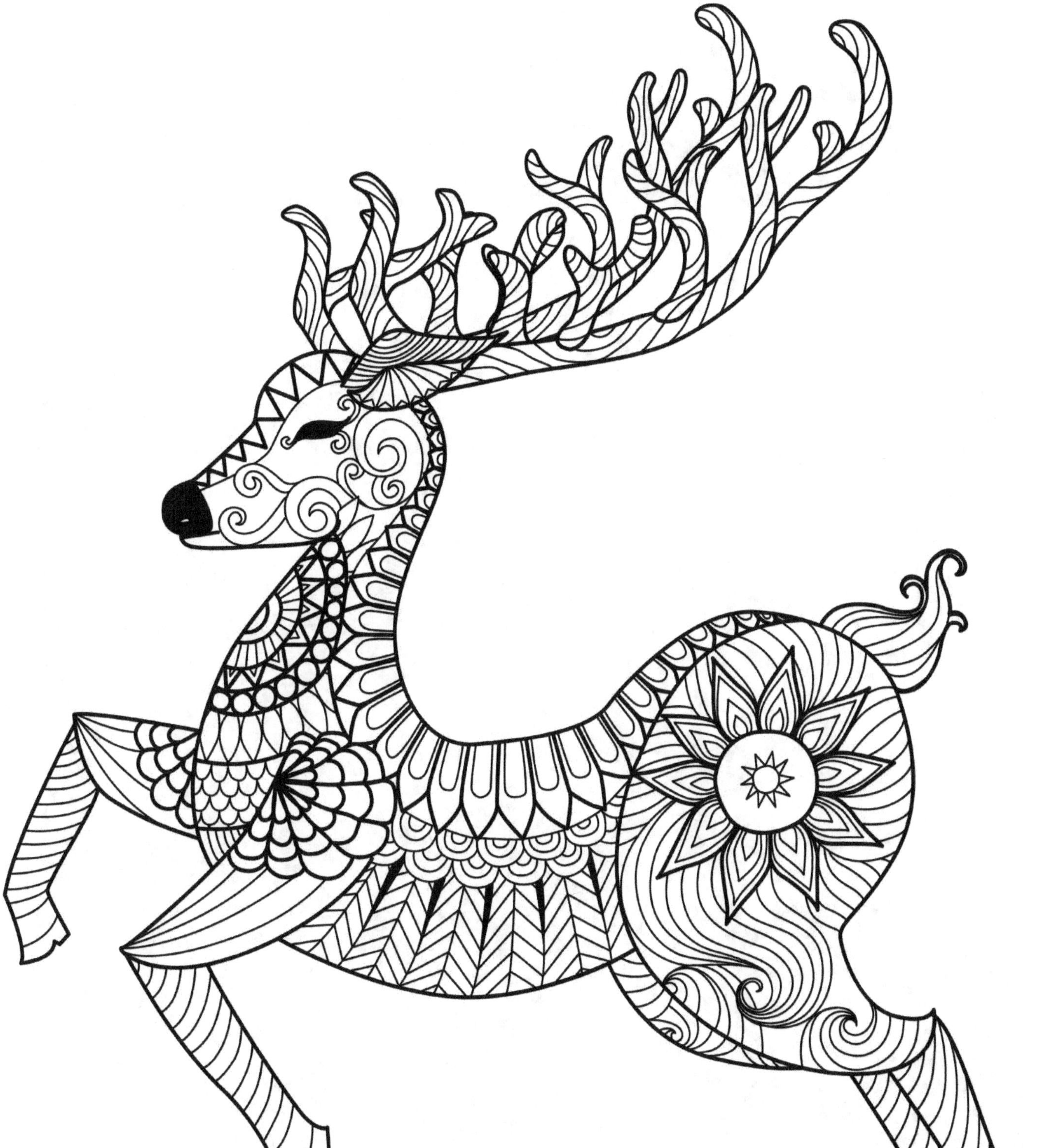

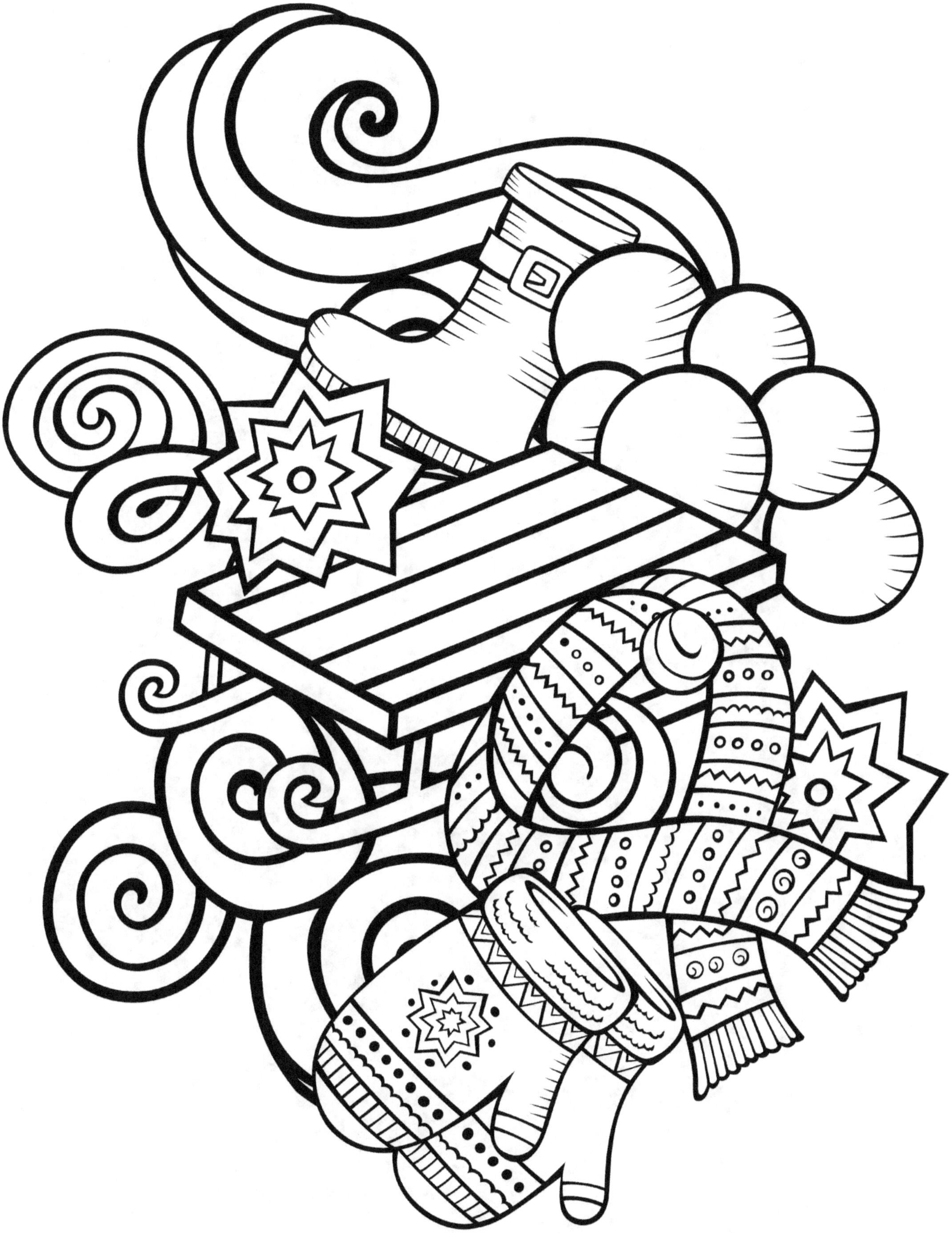

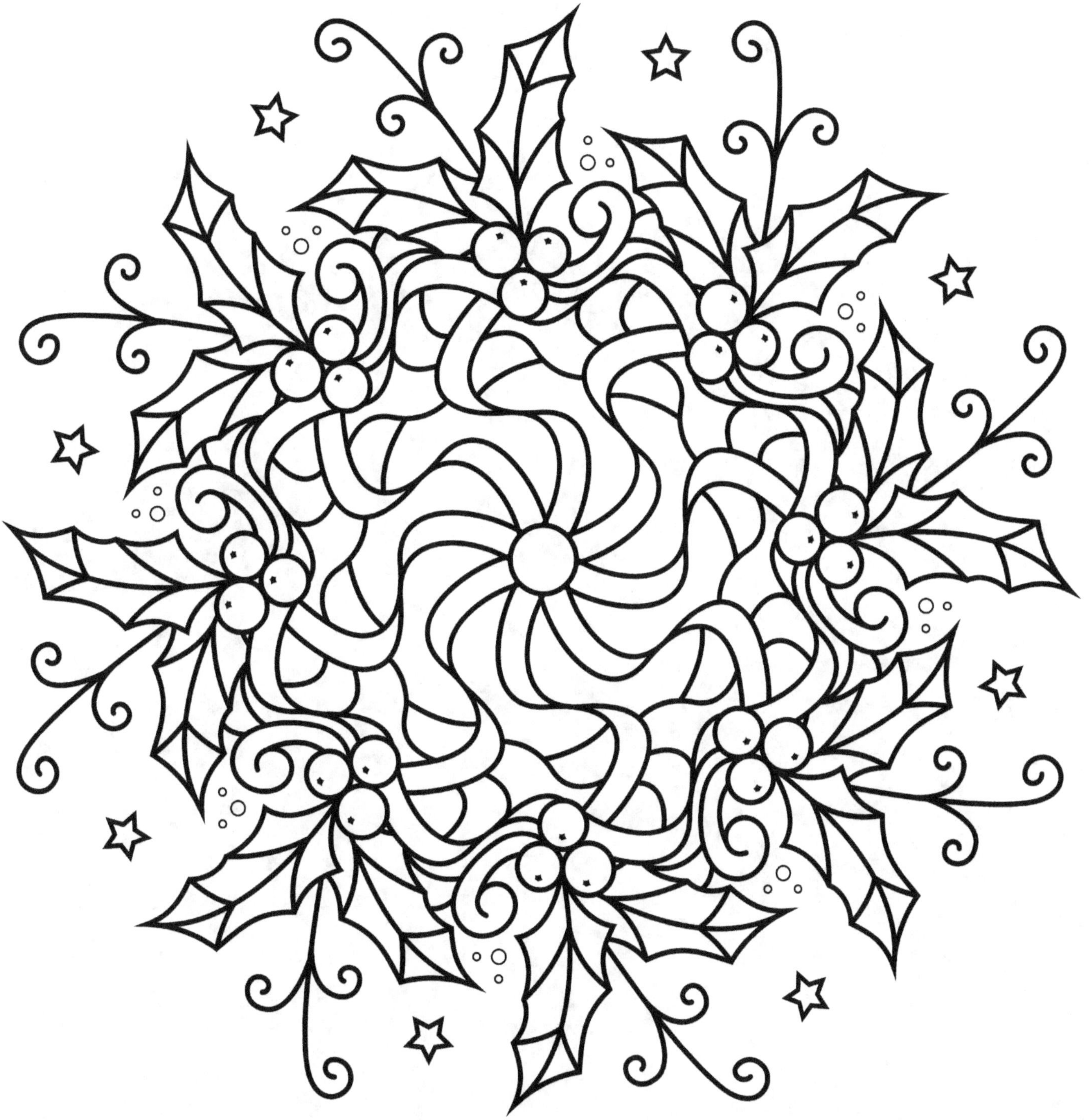

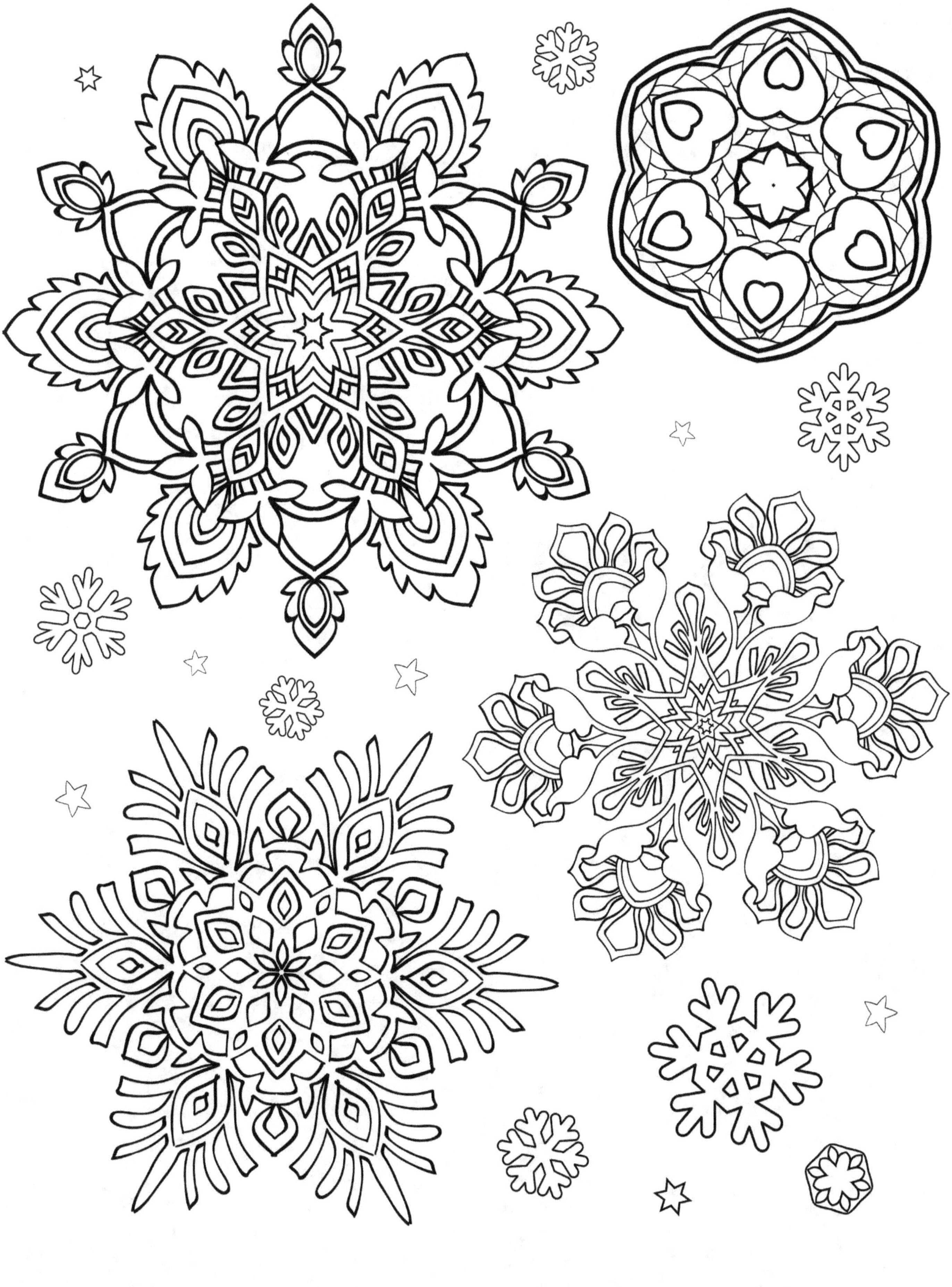

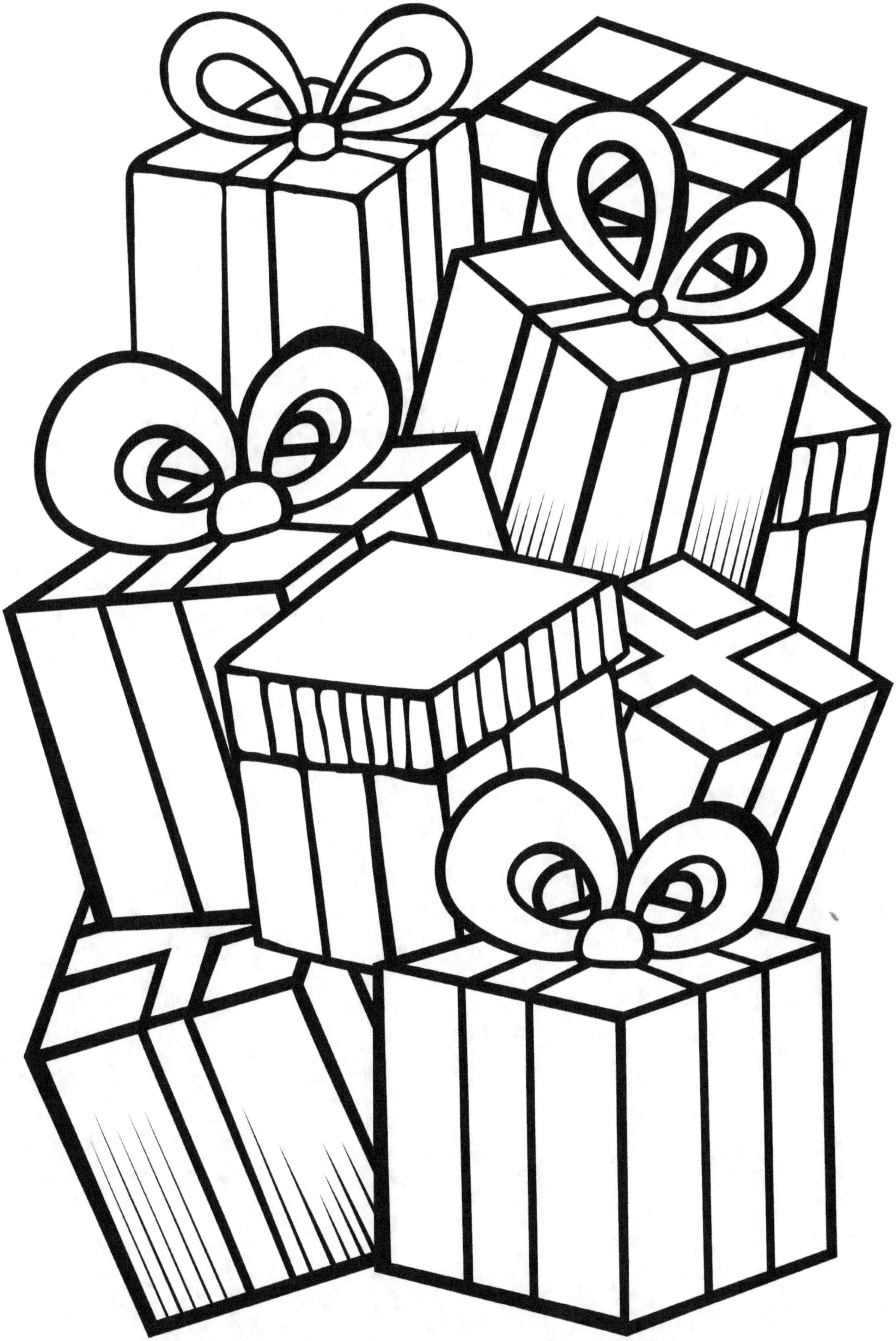

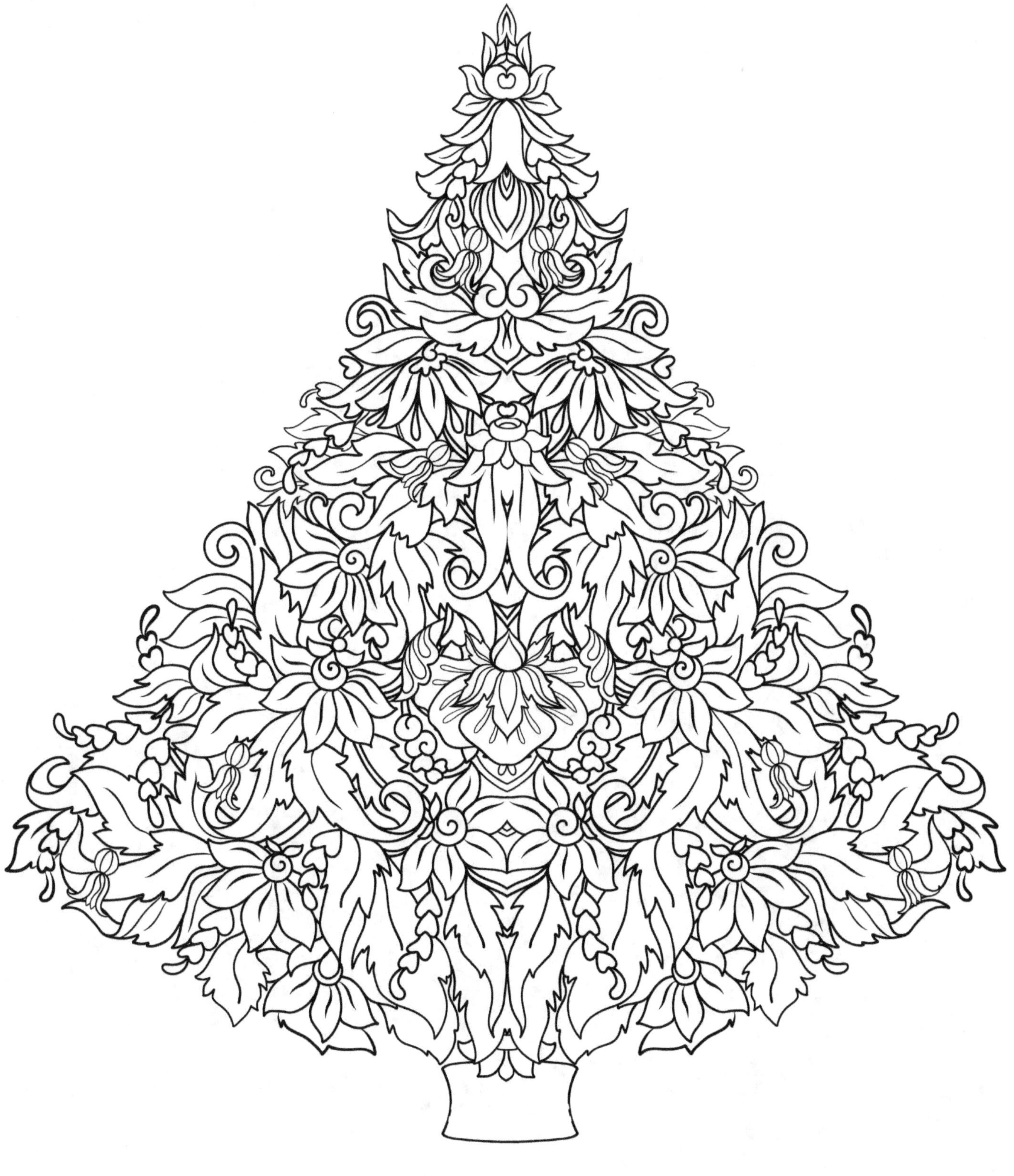

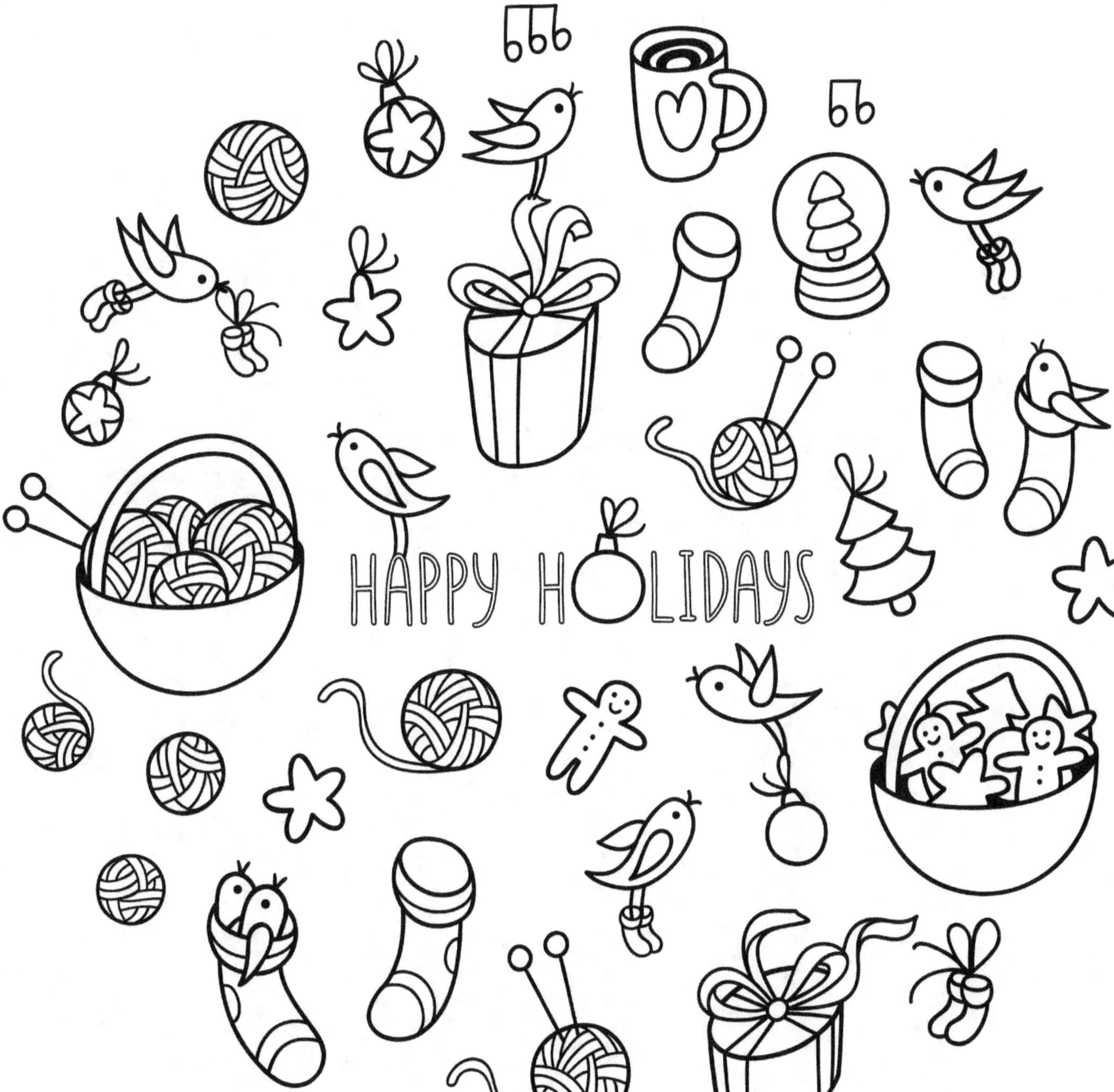
HAPPY HOLIDAYS

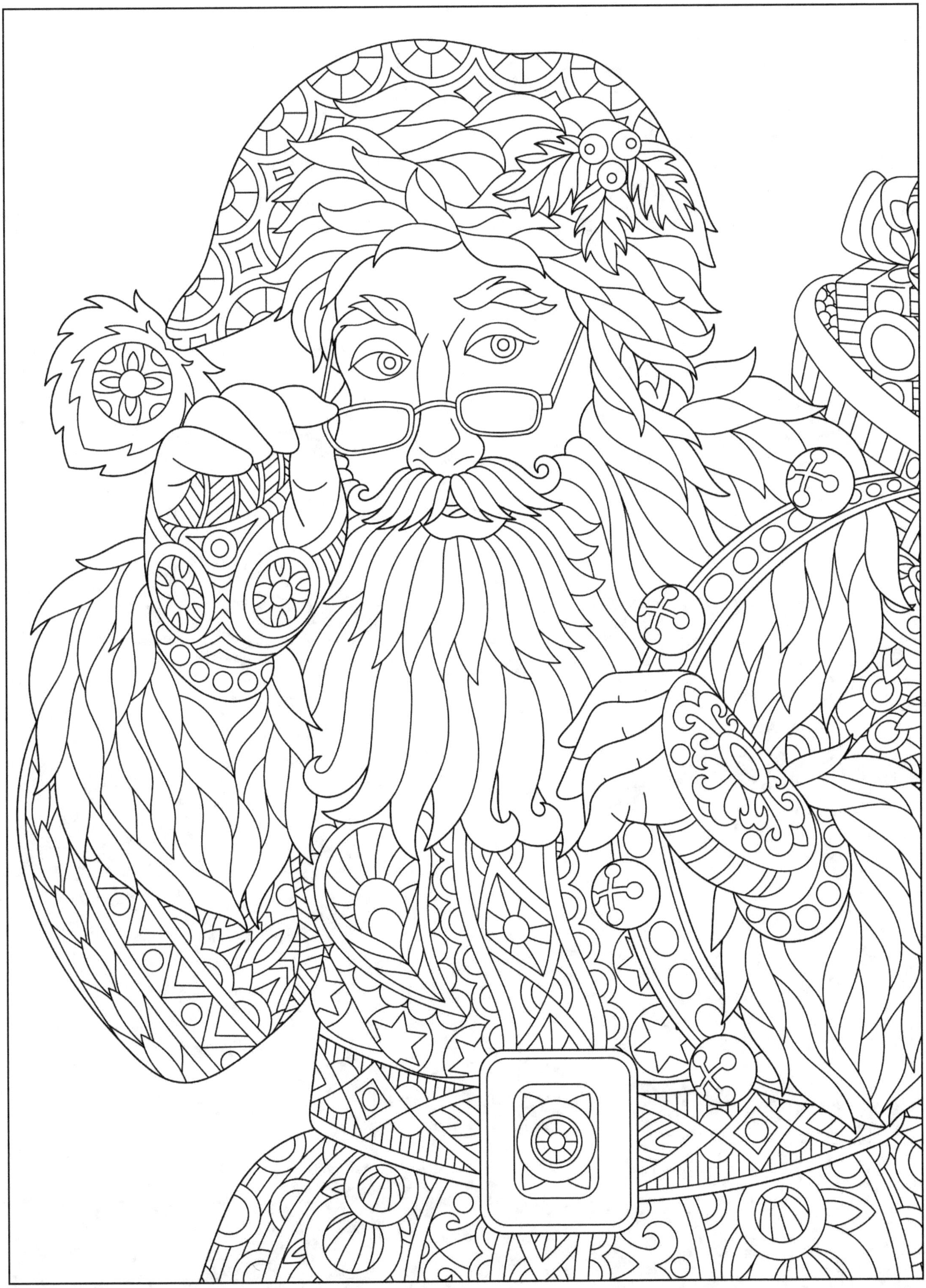

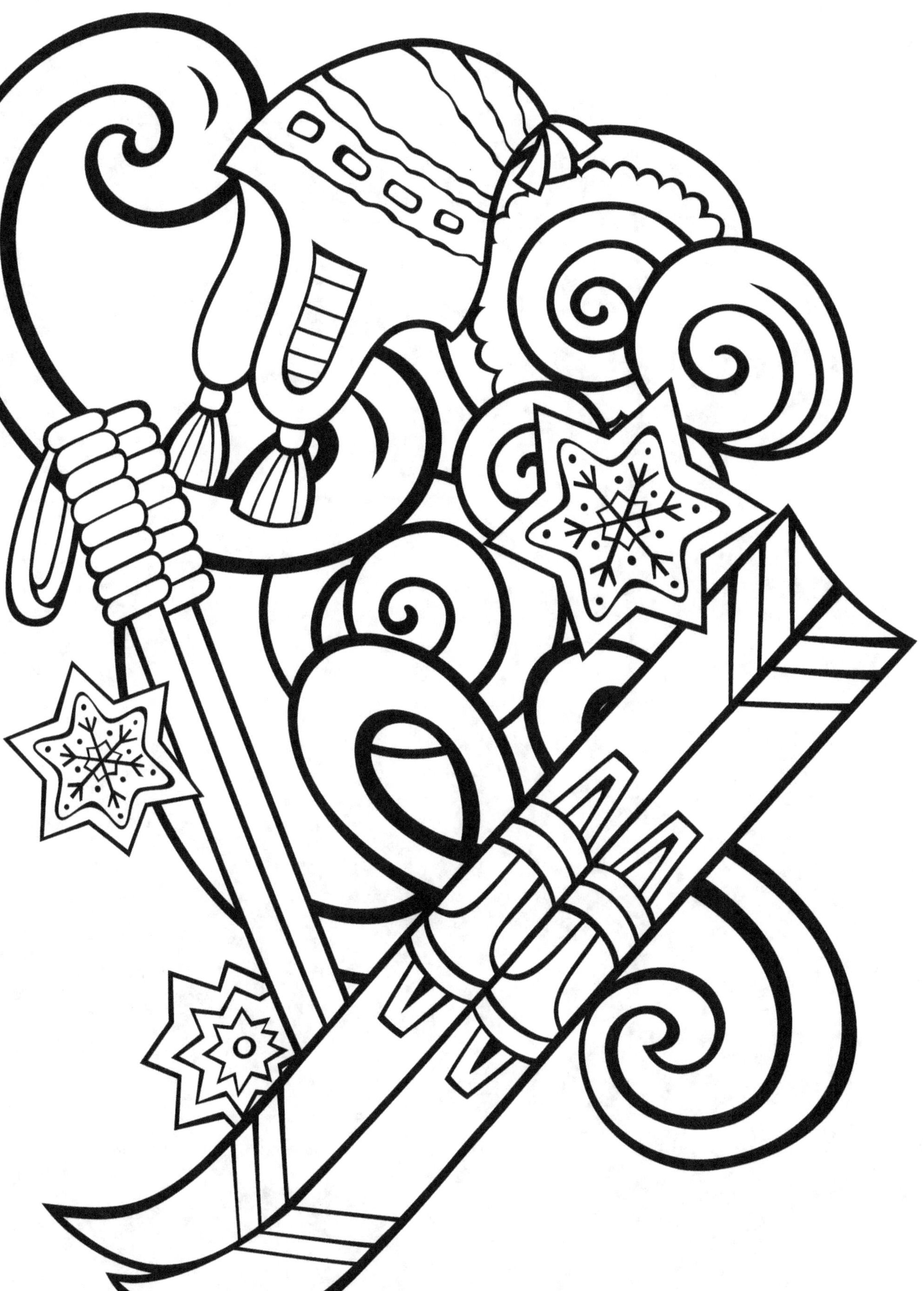

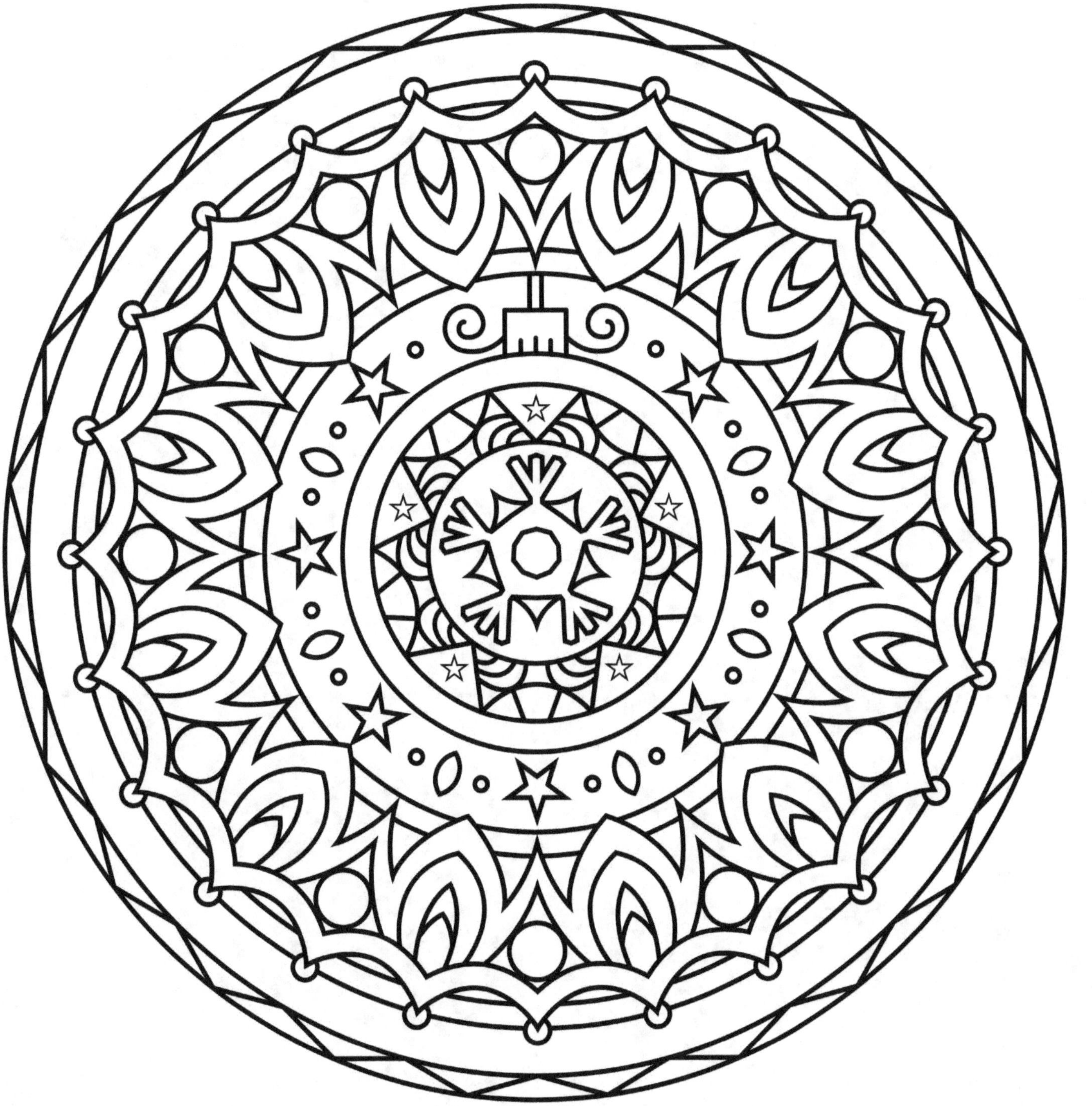

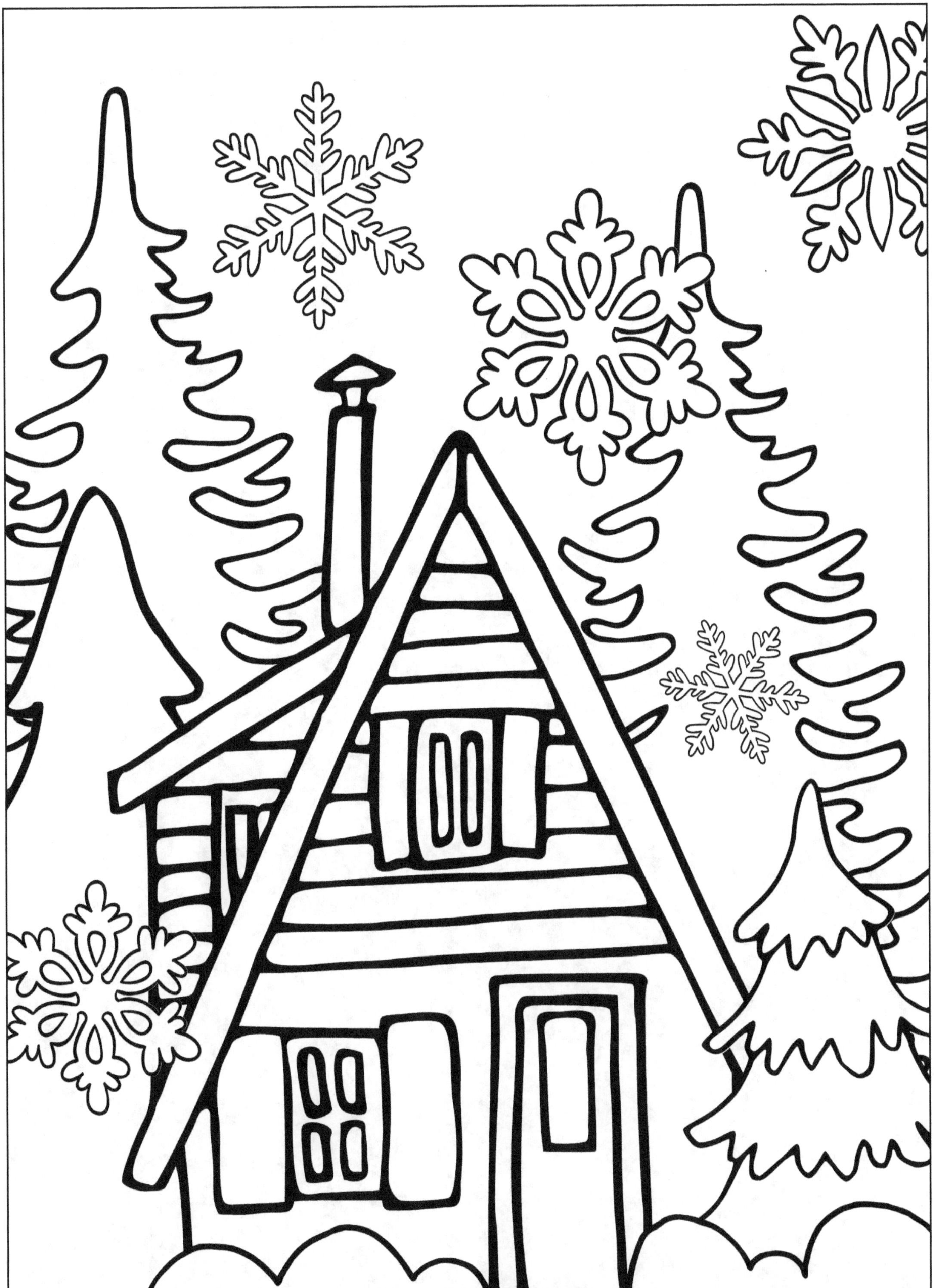

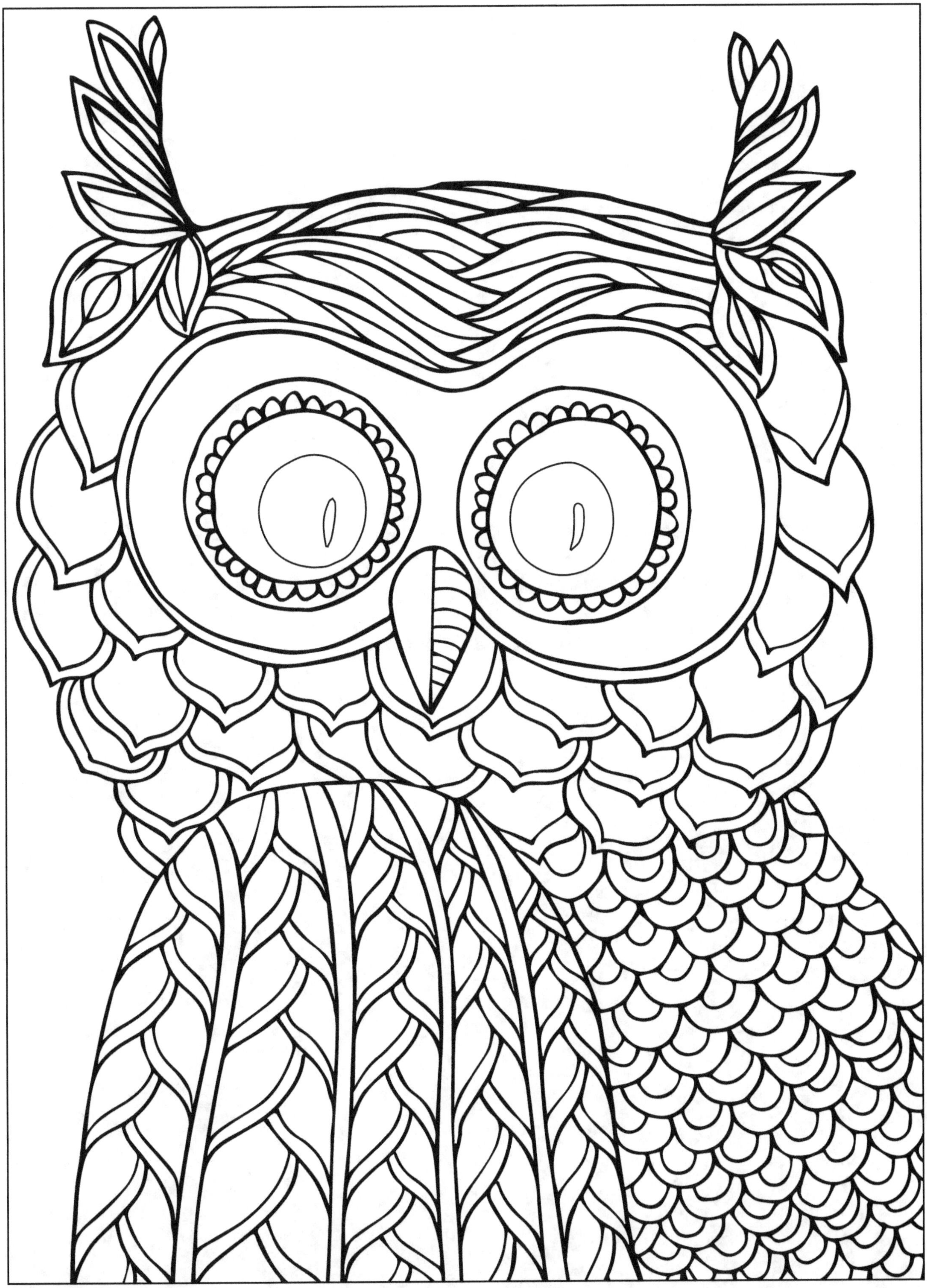

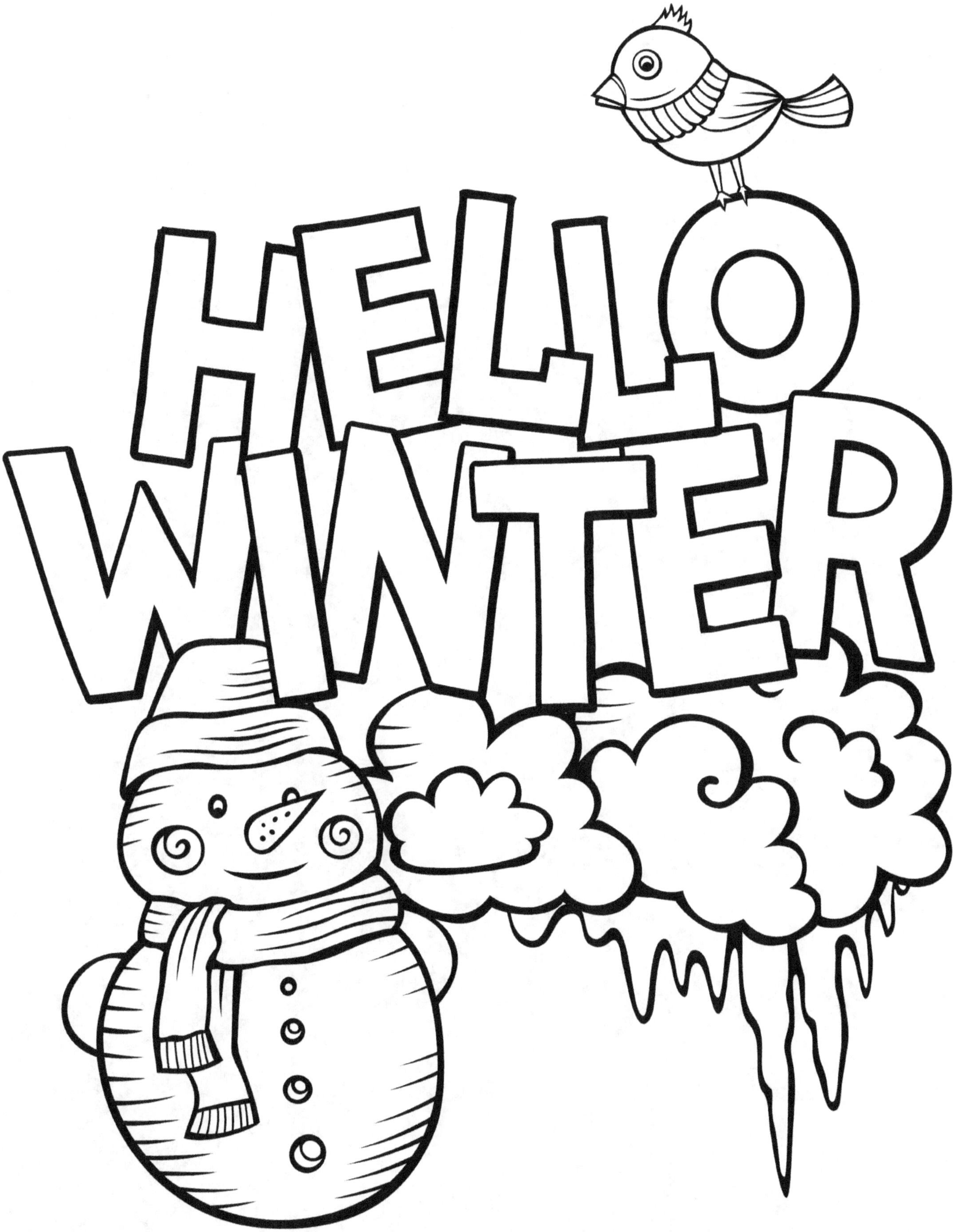
HELLO
WINTER

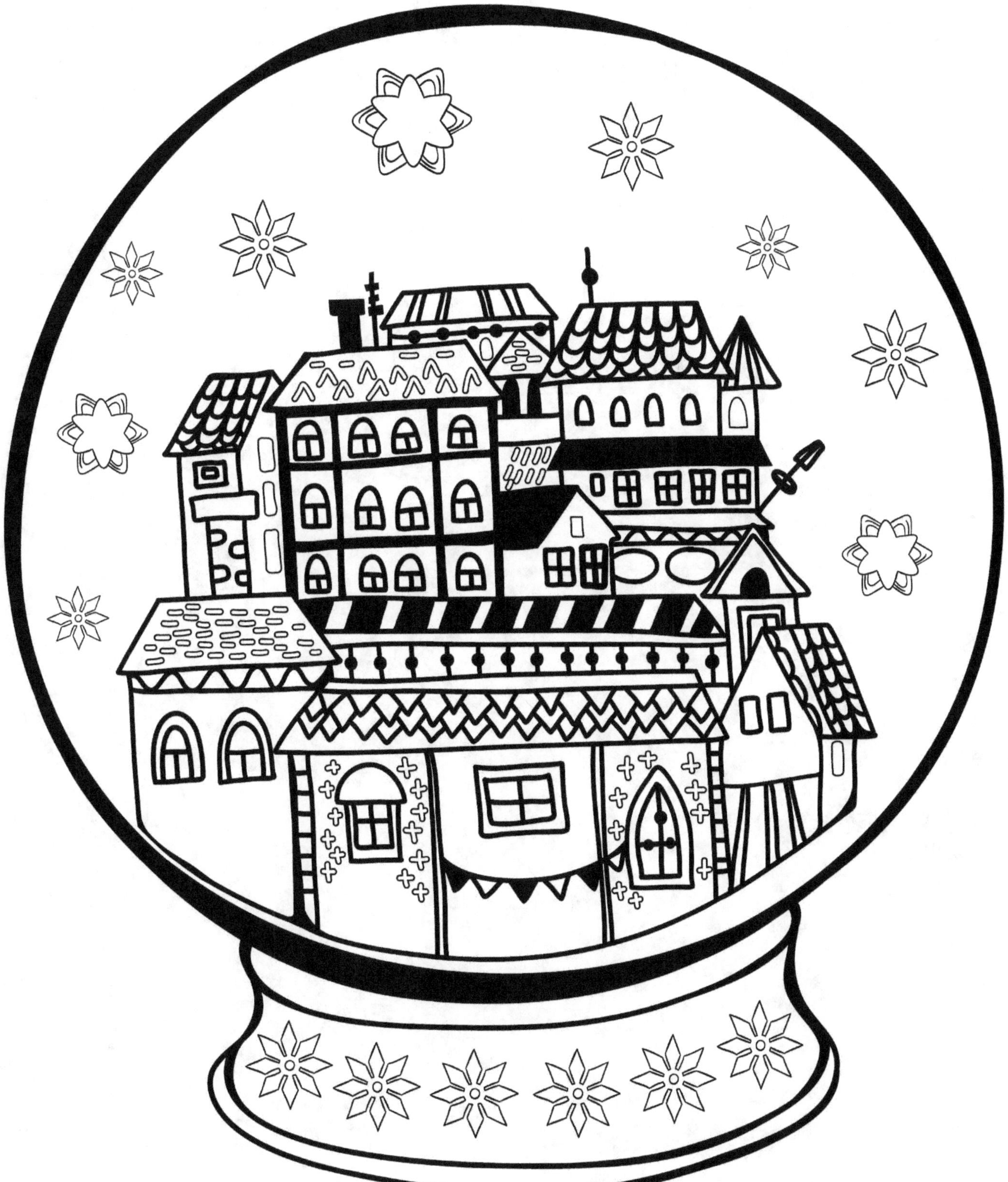

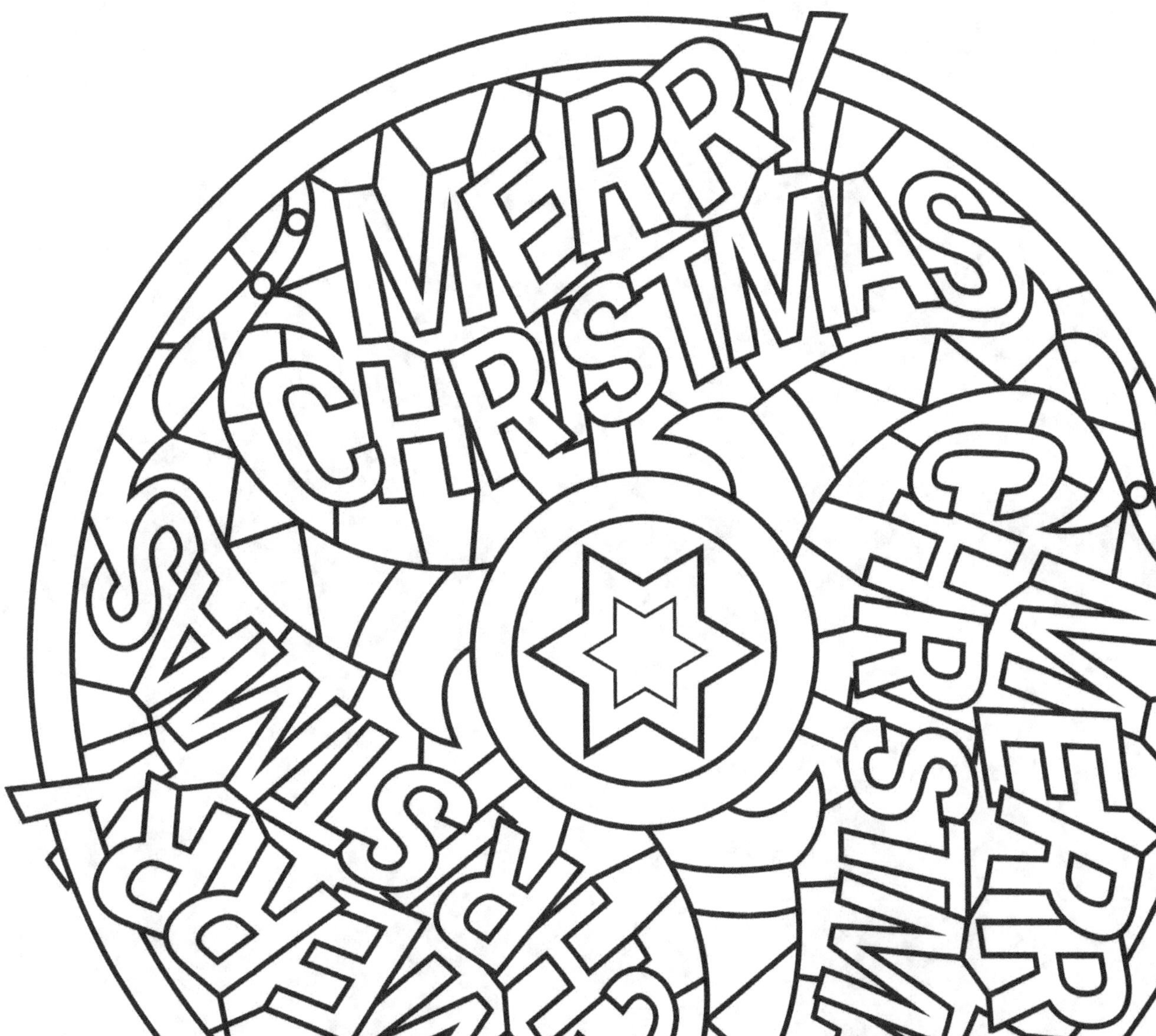
MERRY CHRISTMAS
MERRY CHRISTMAS
MERRY CHRISTMAS

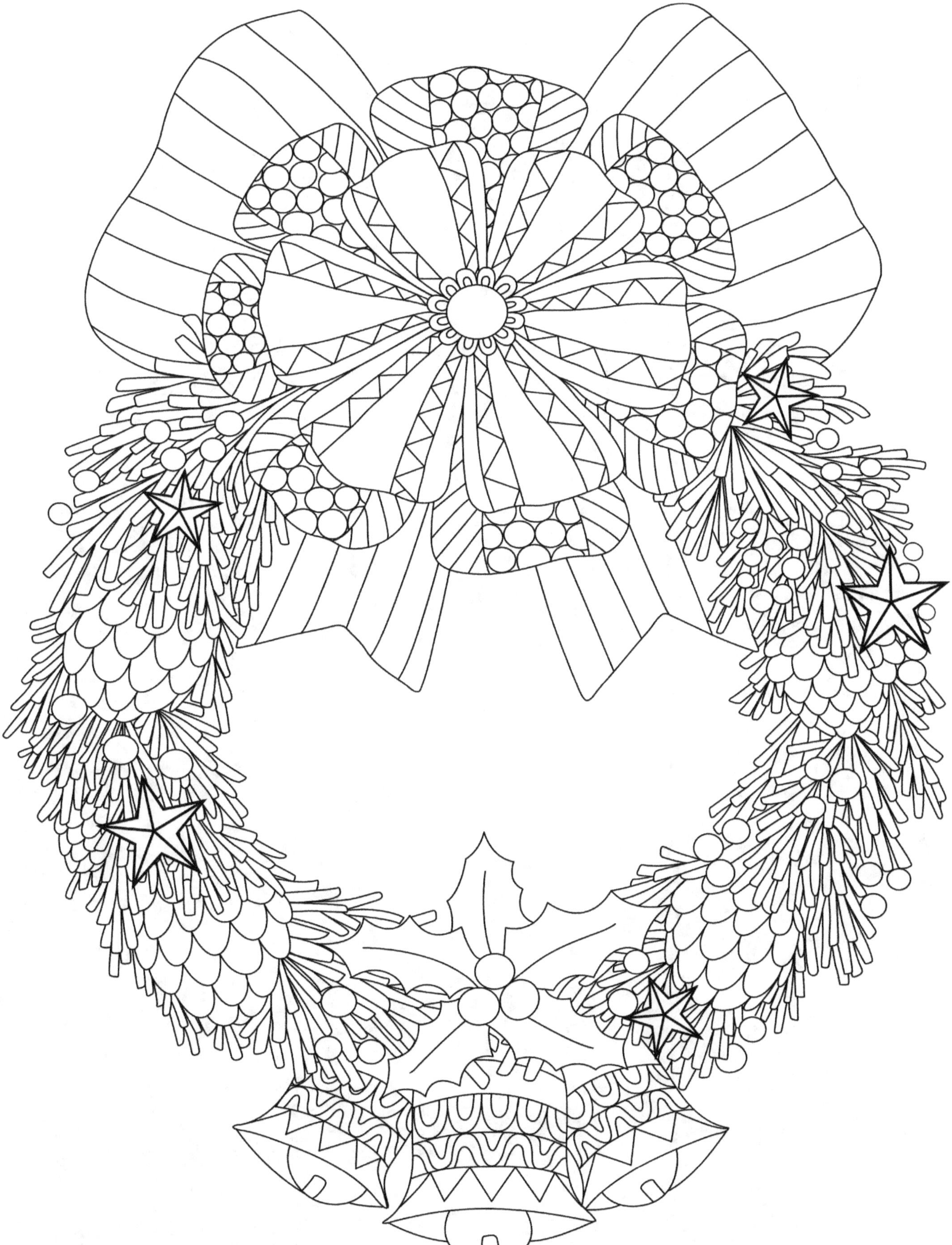

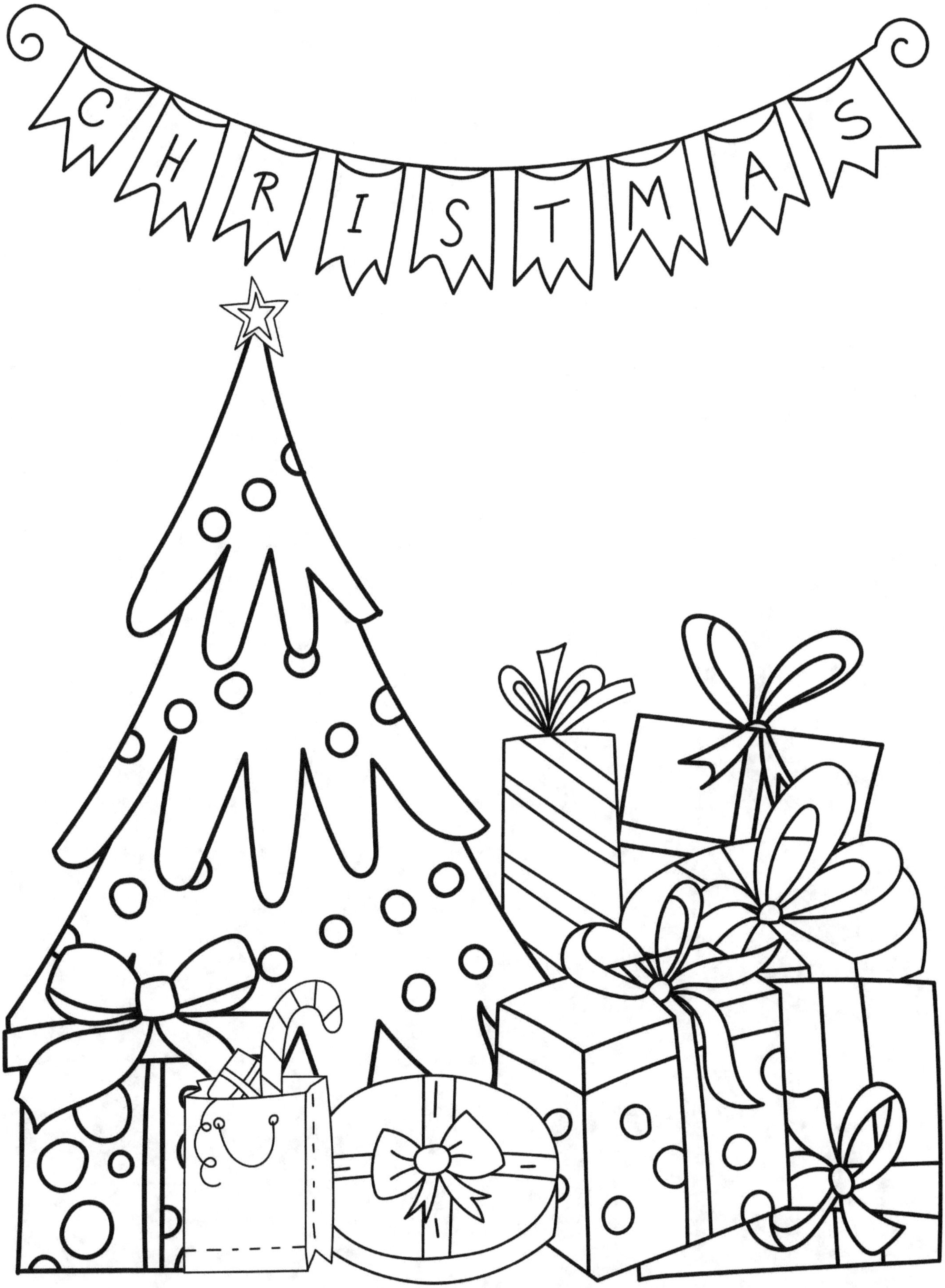
CHRISTMAS

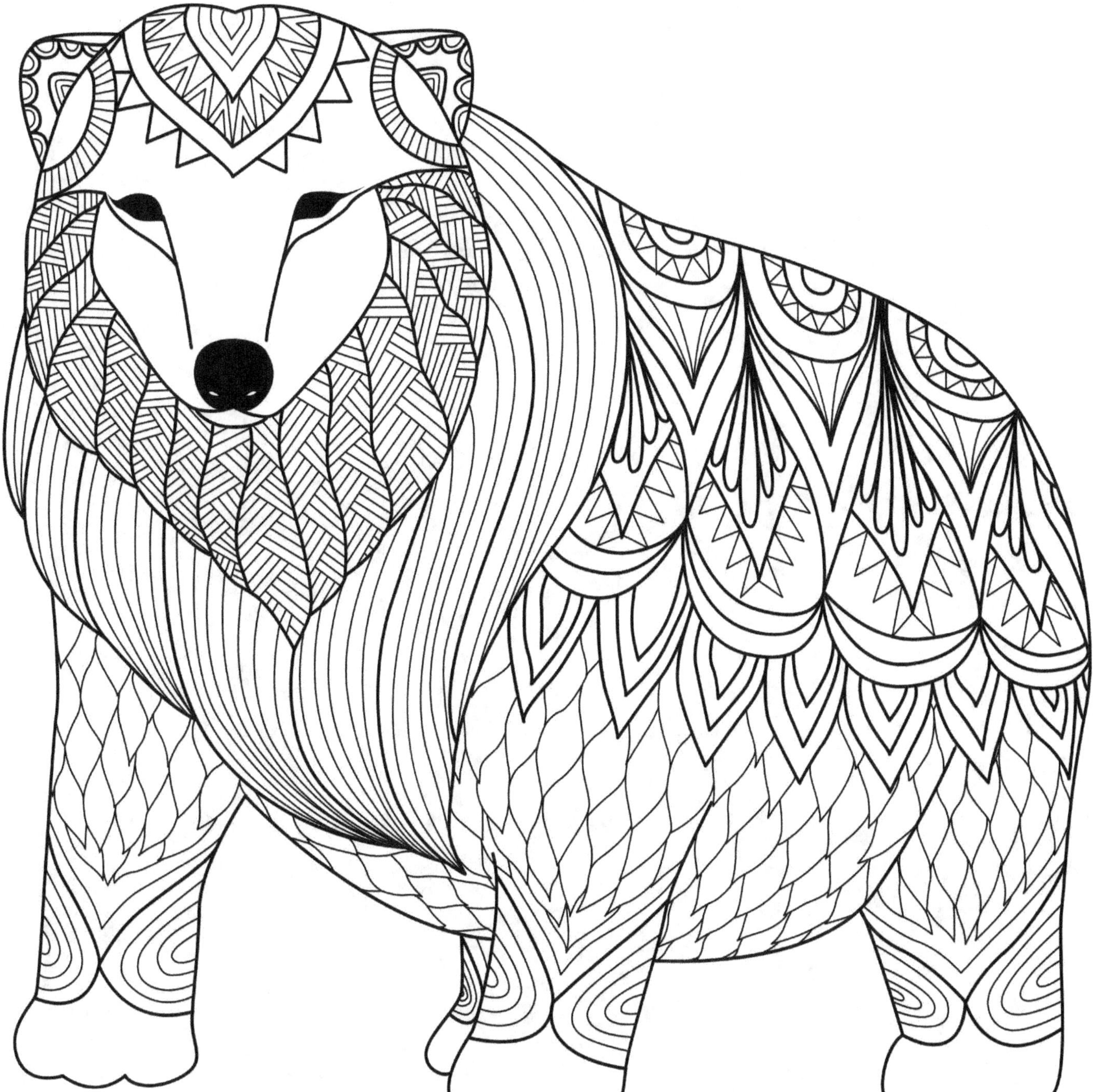

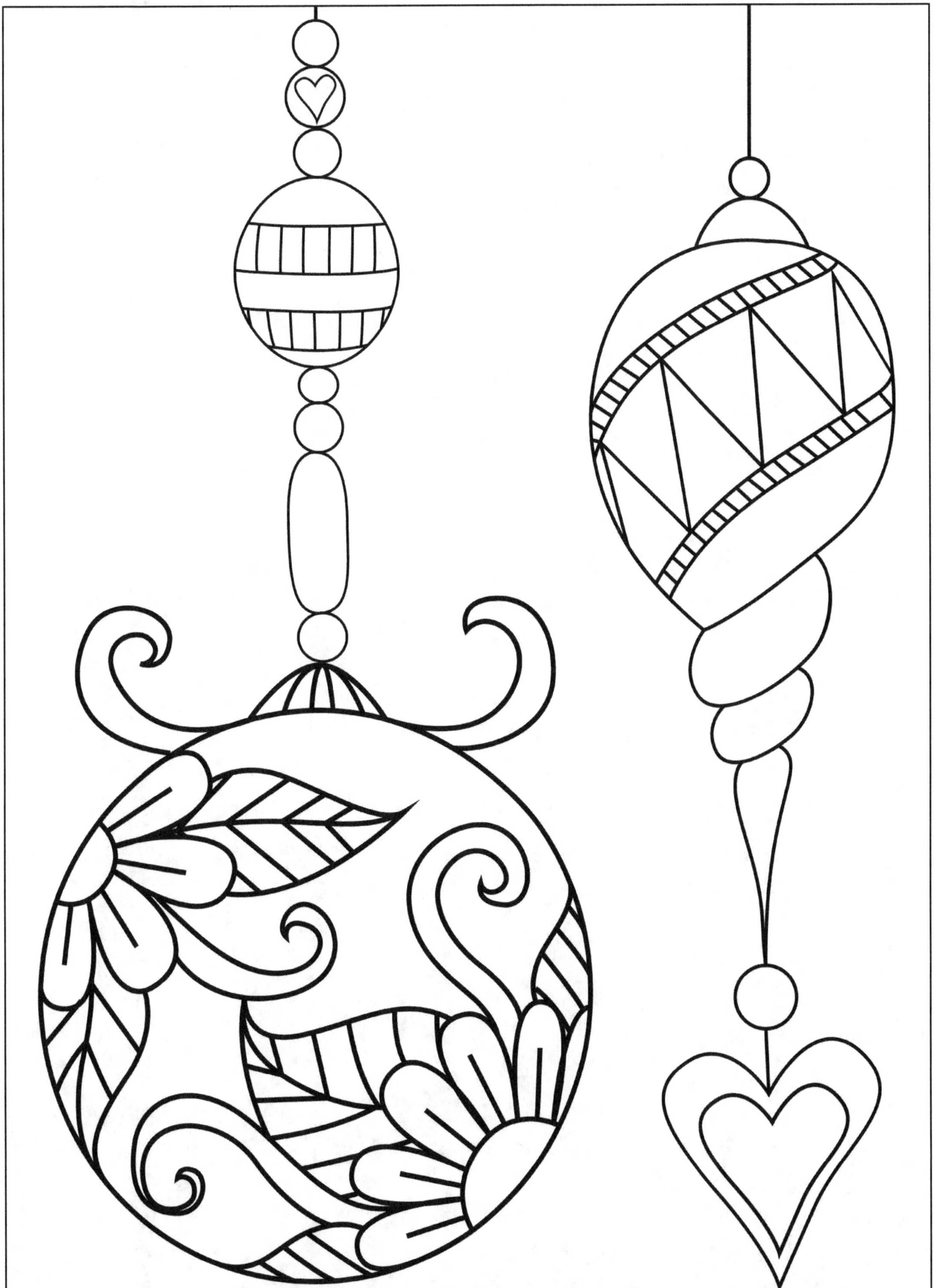

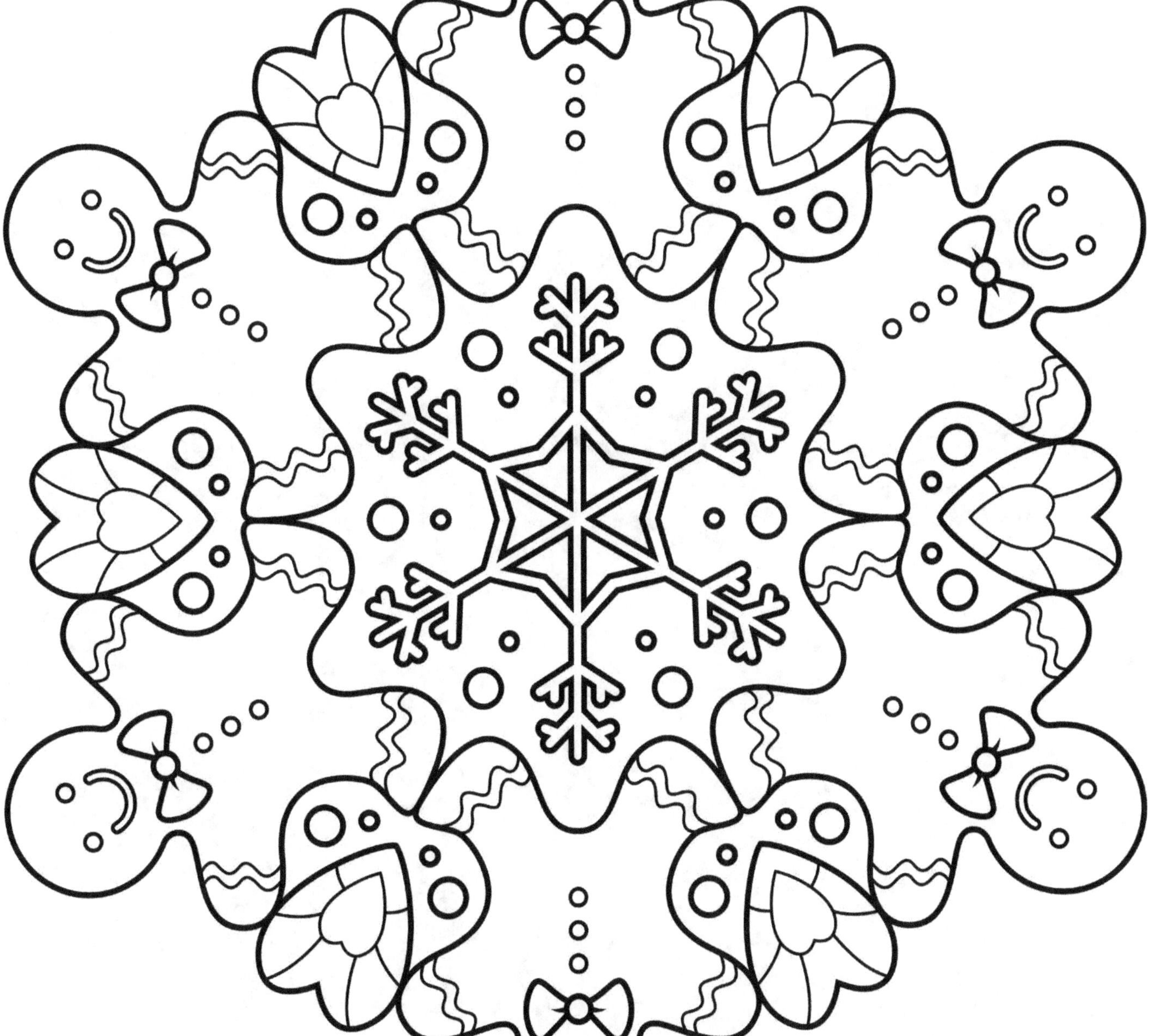

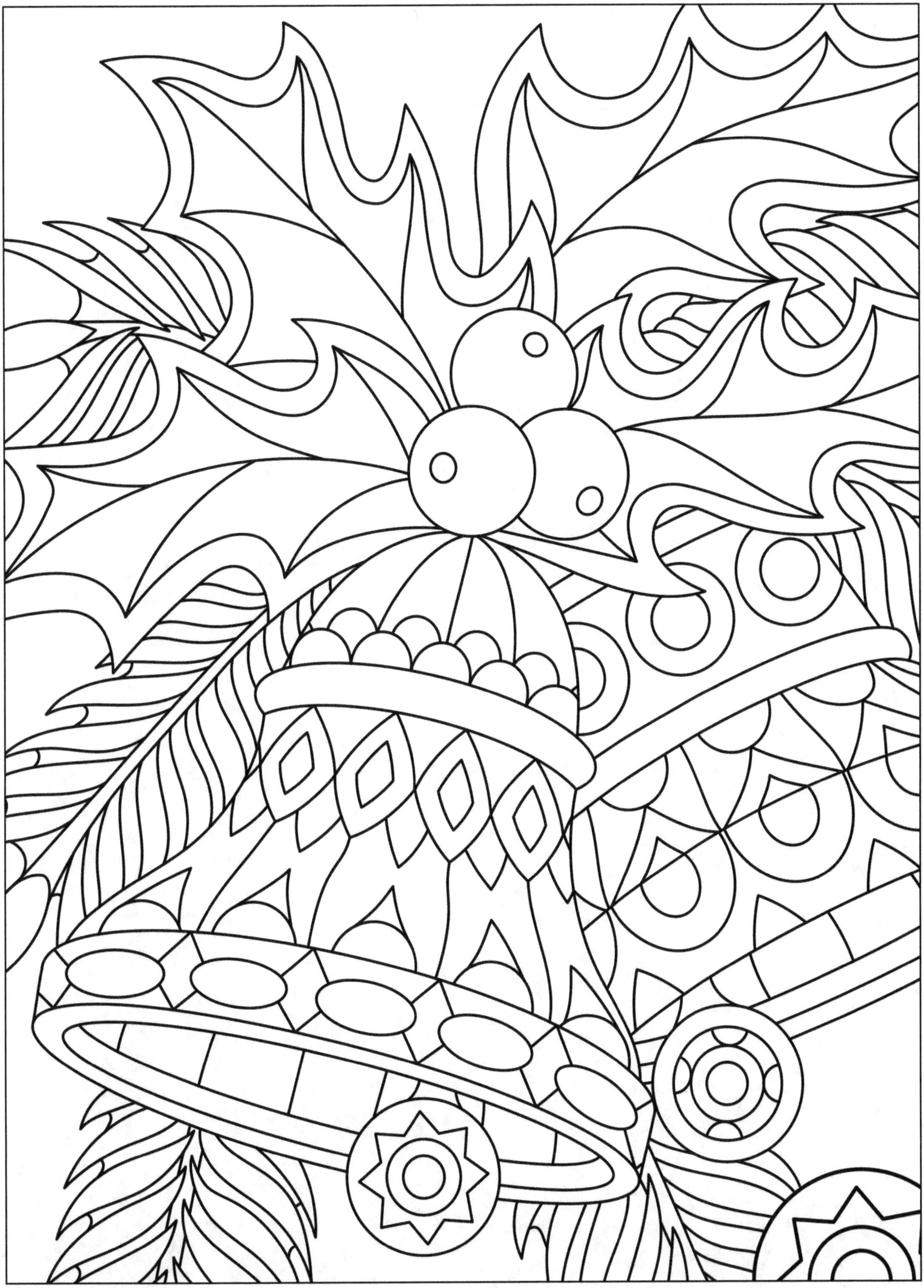

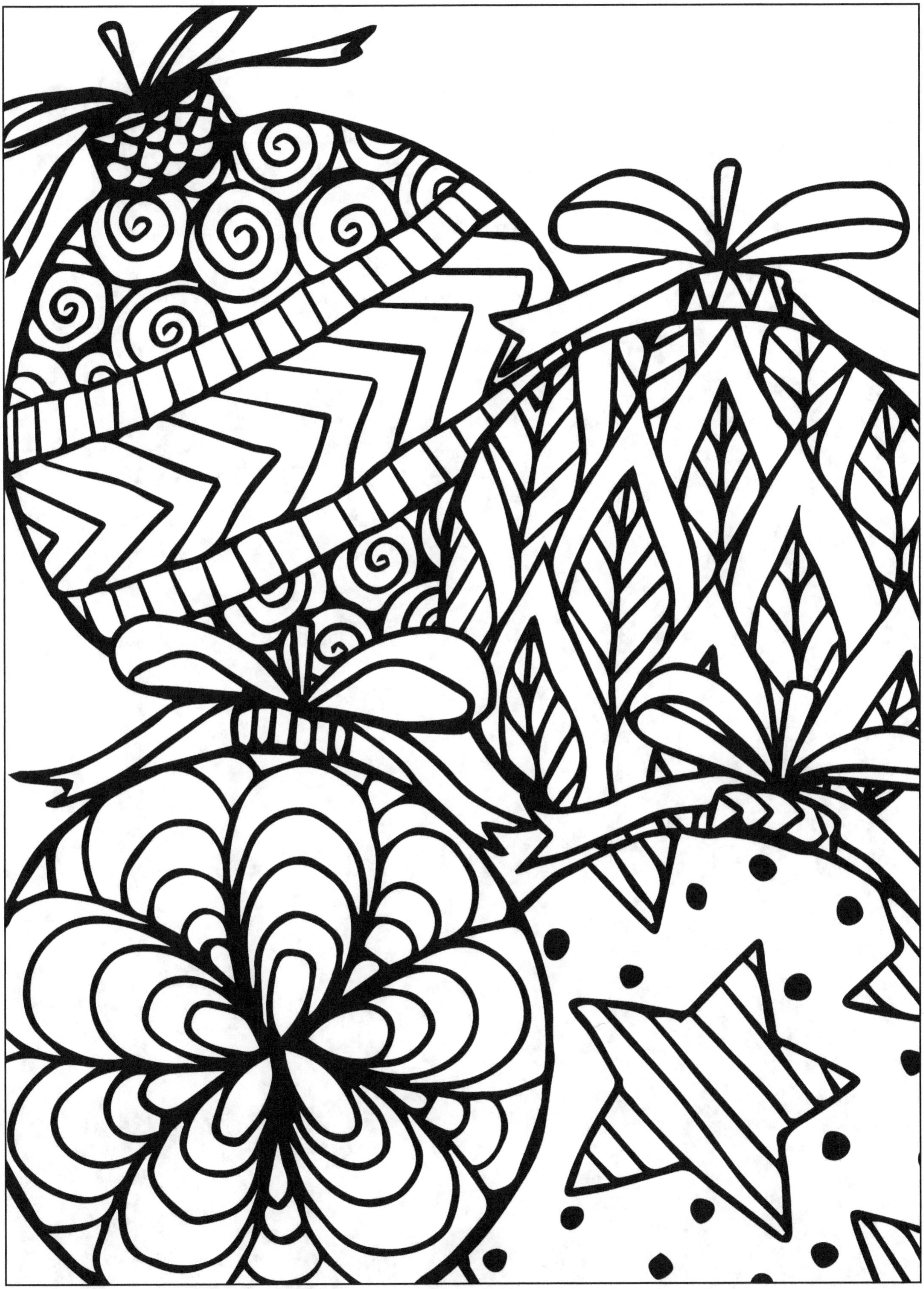

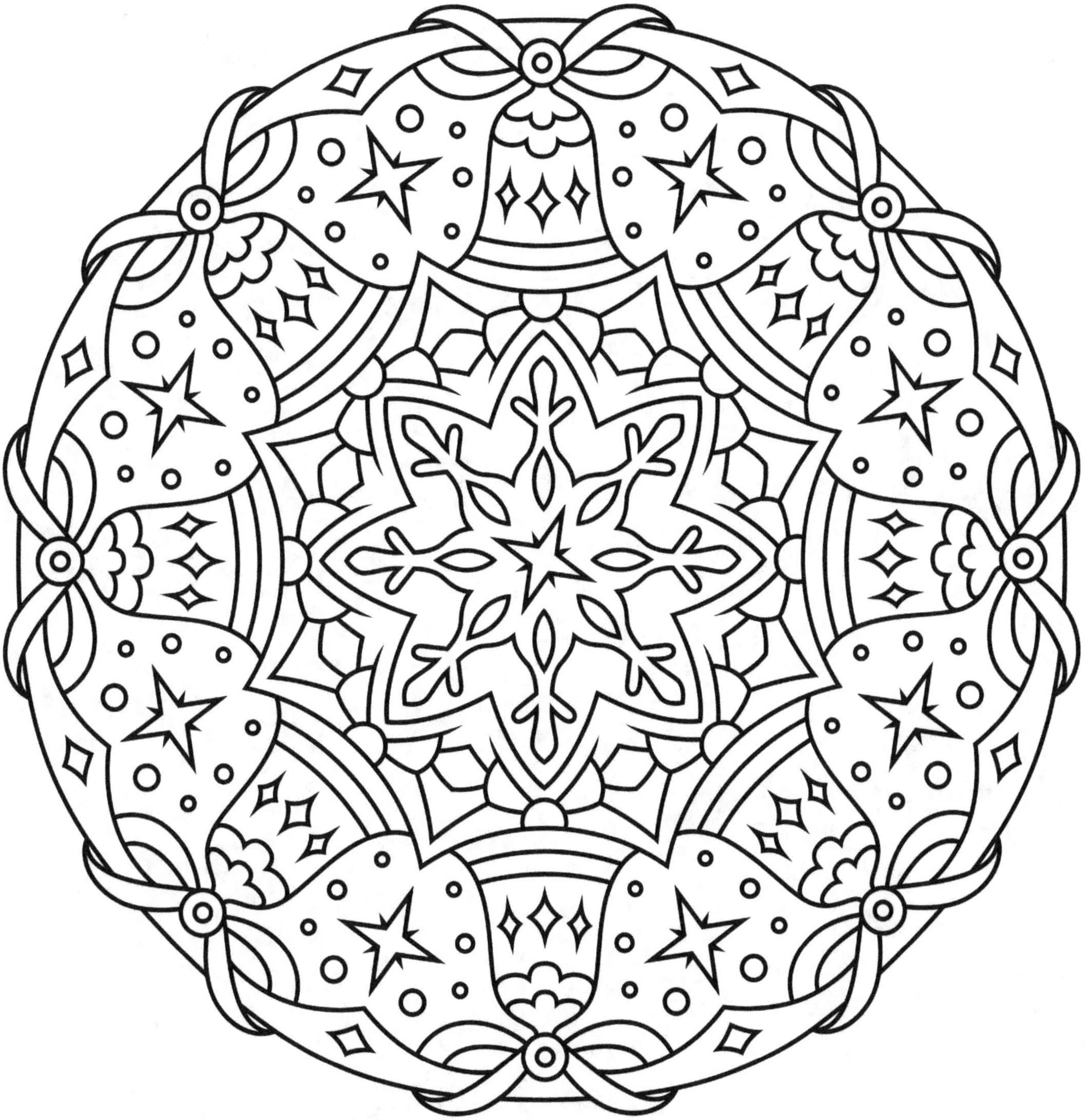

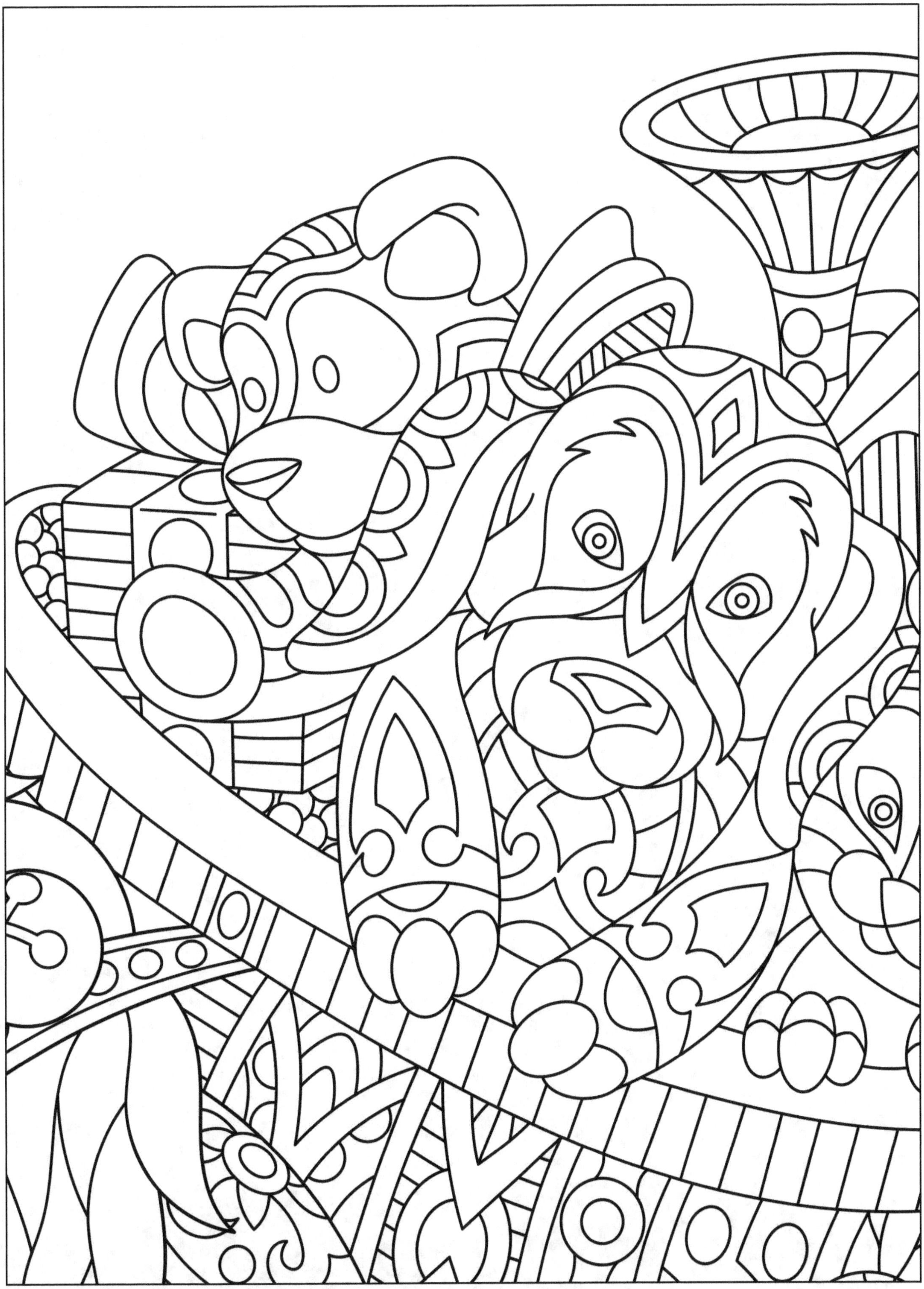

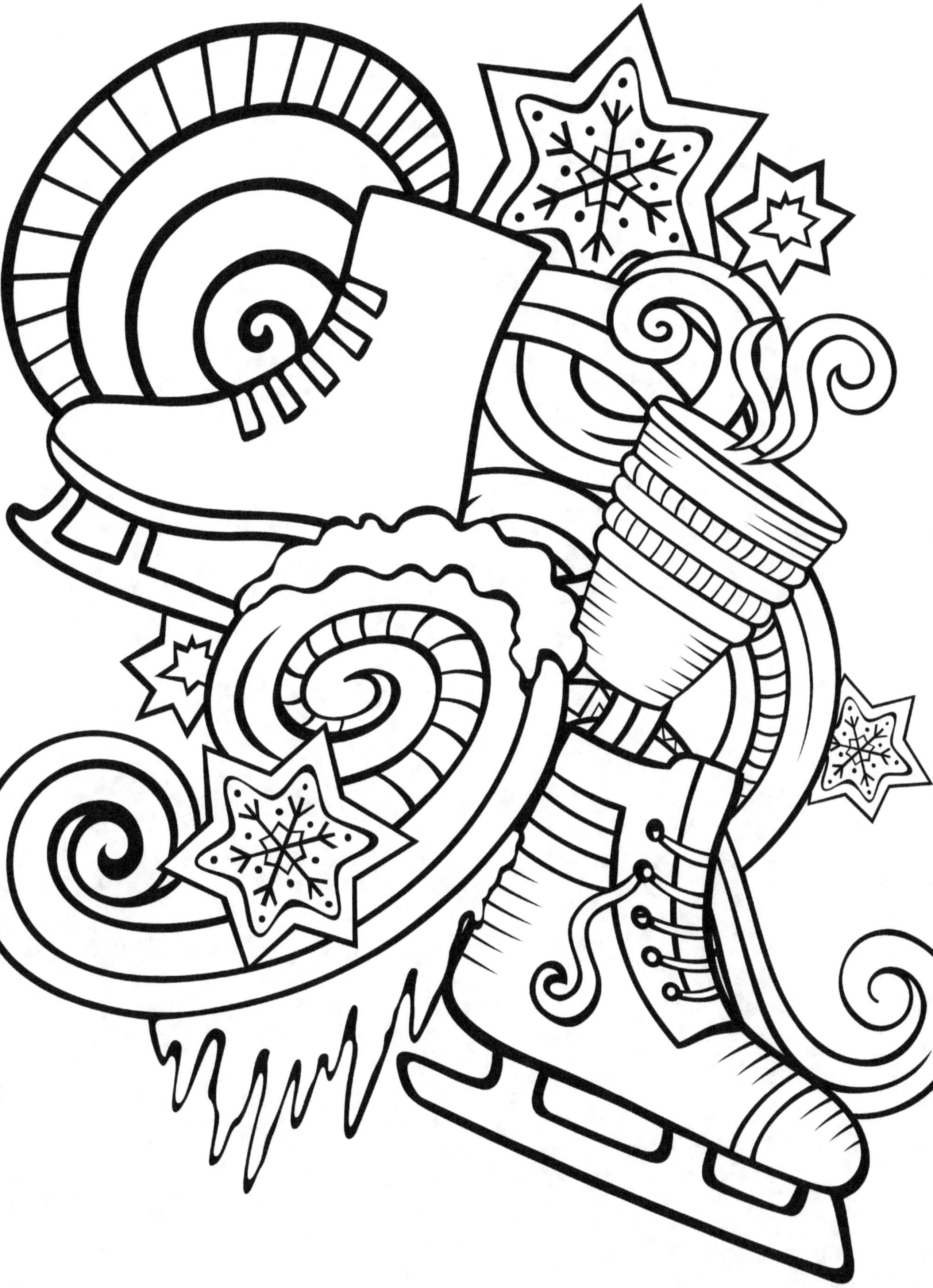

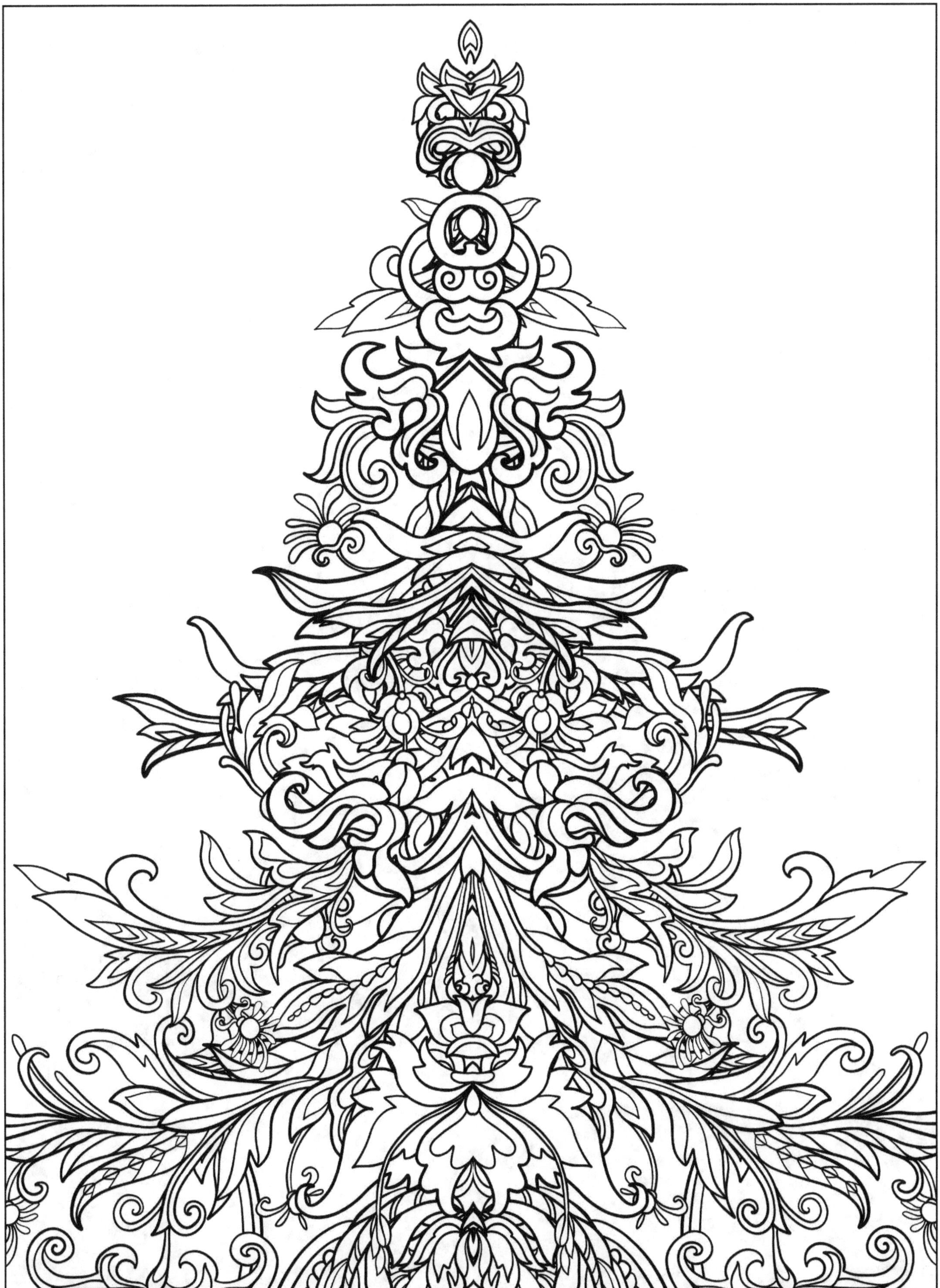

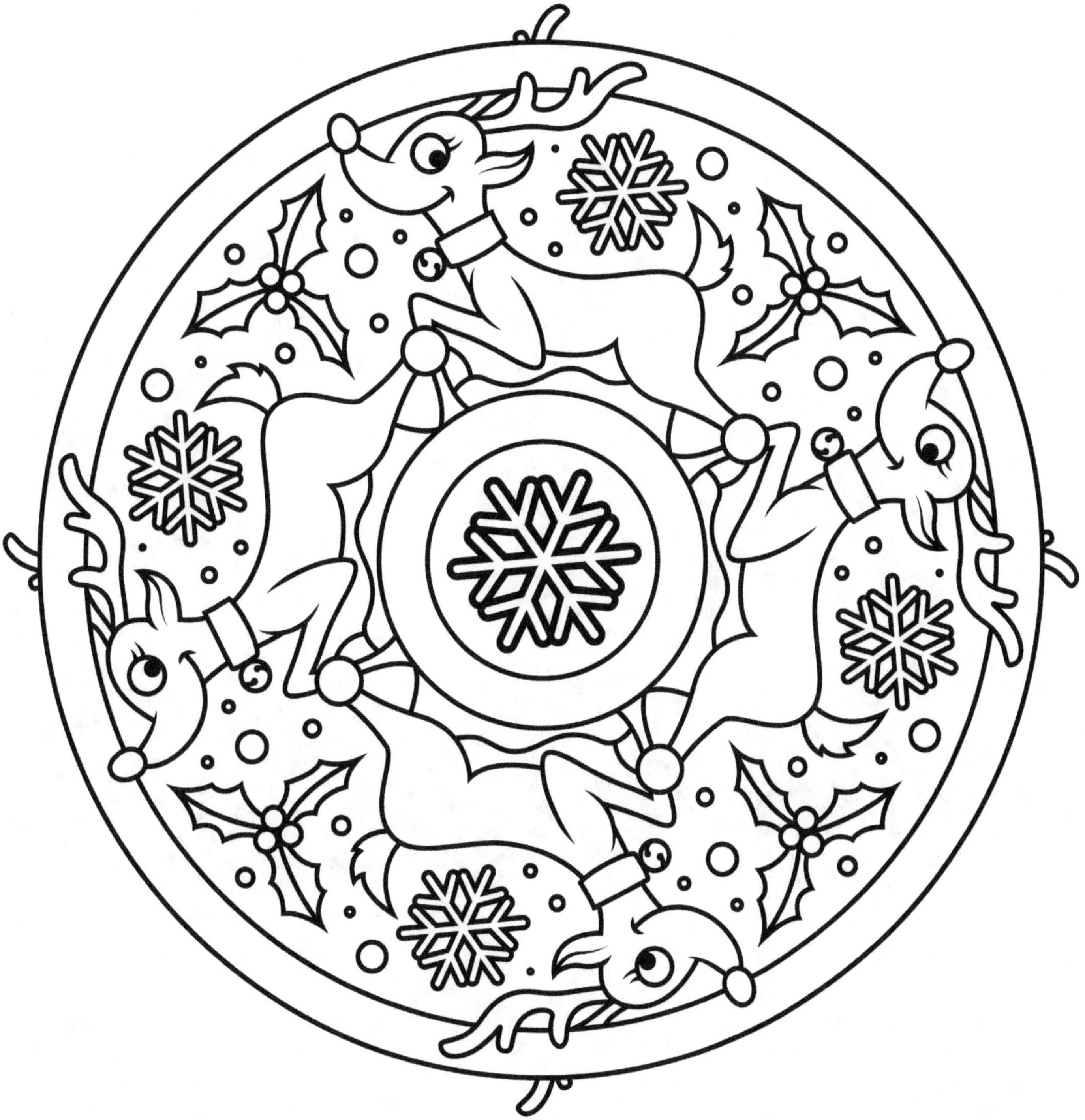

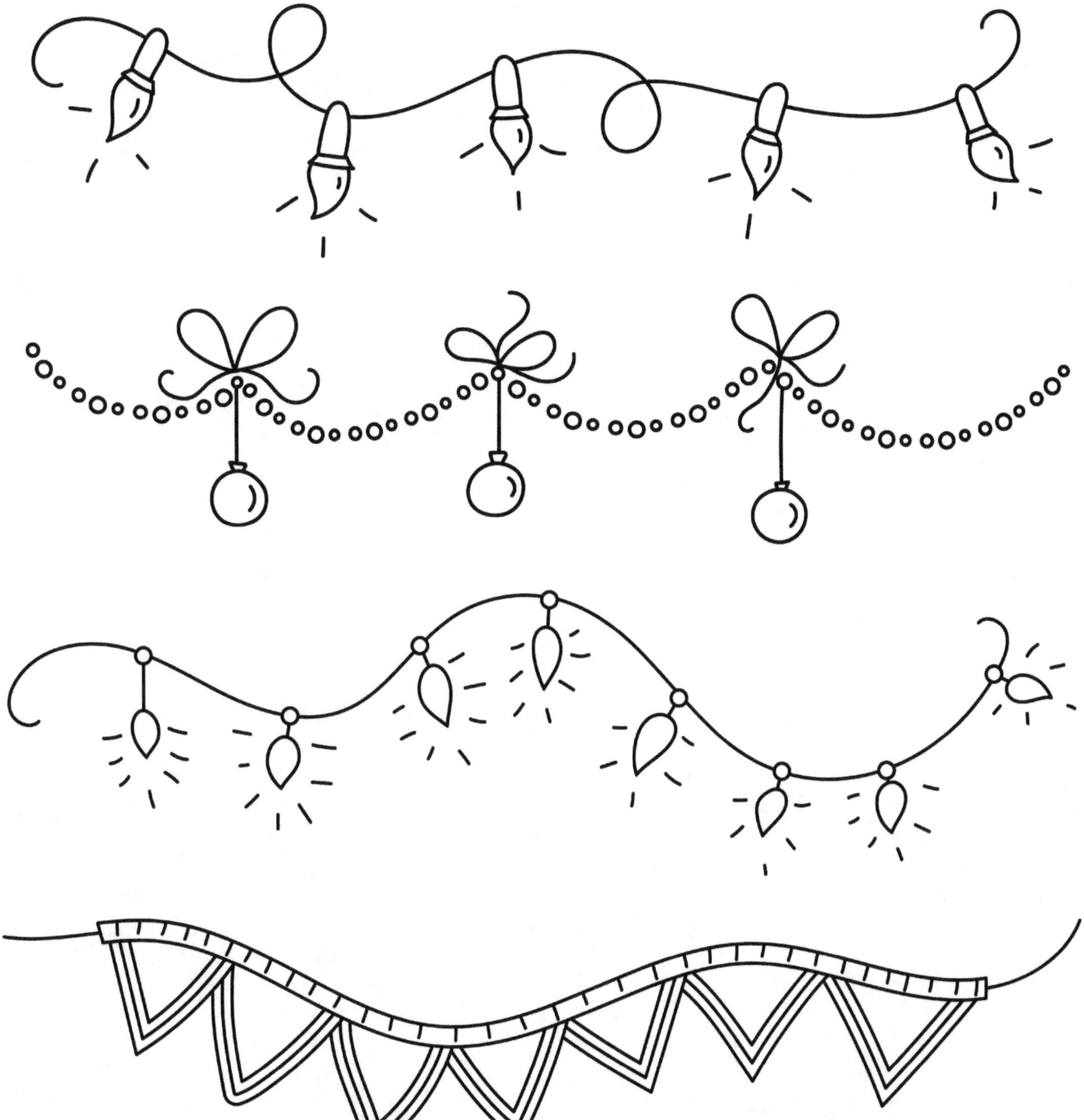

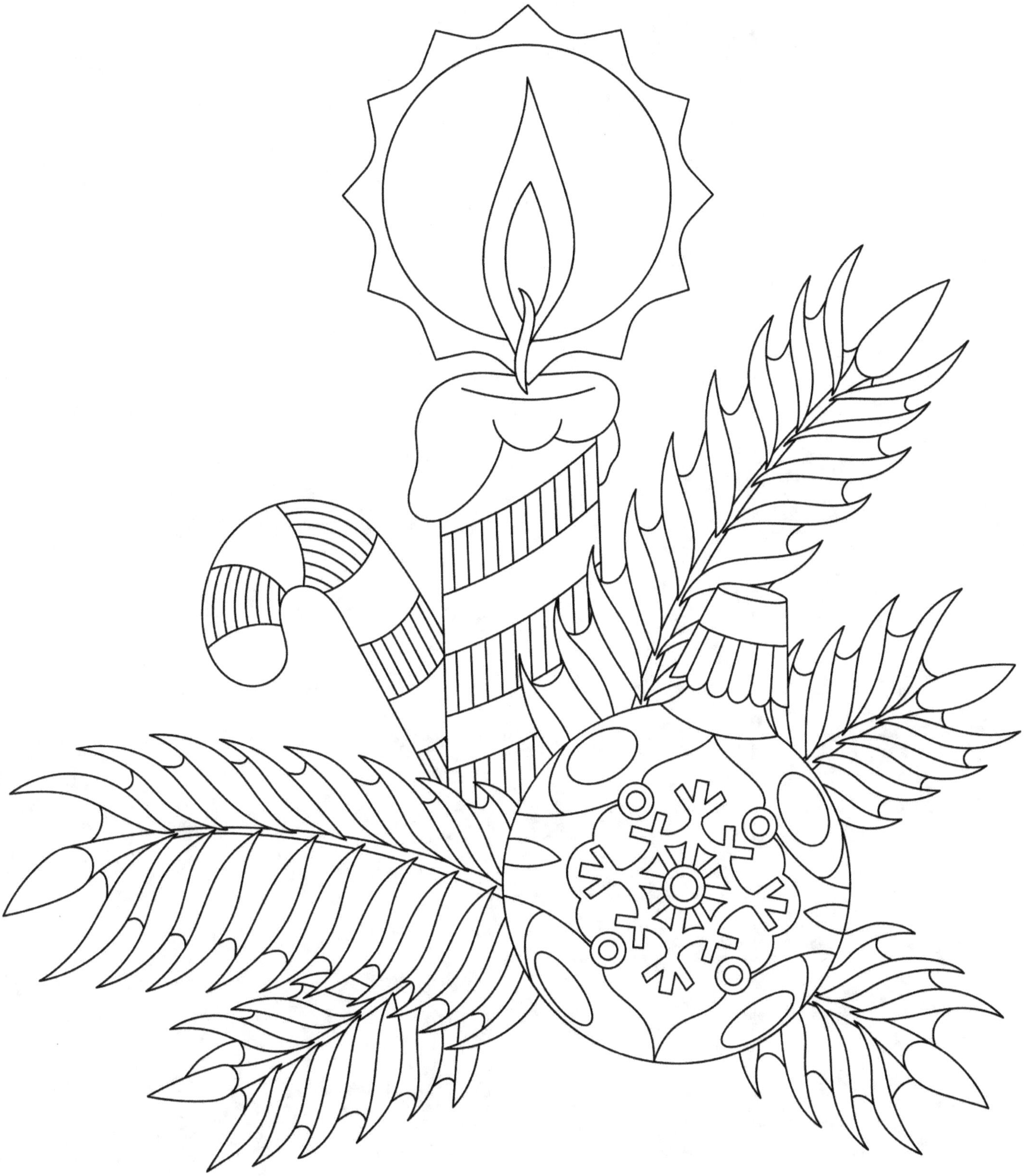

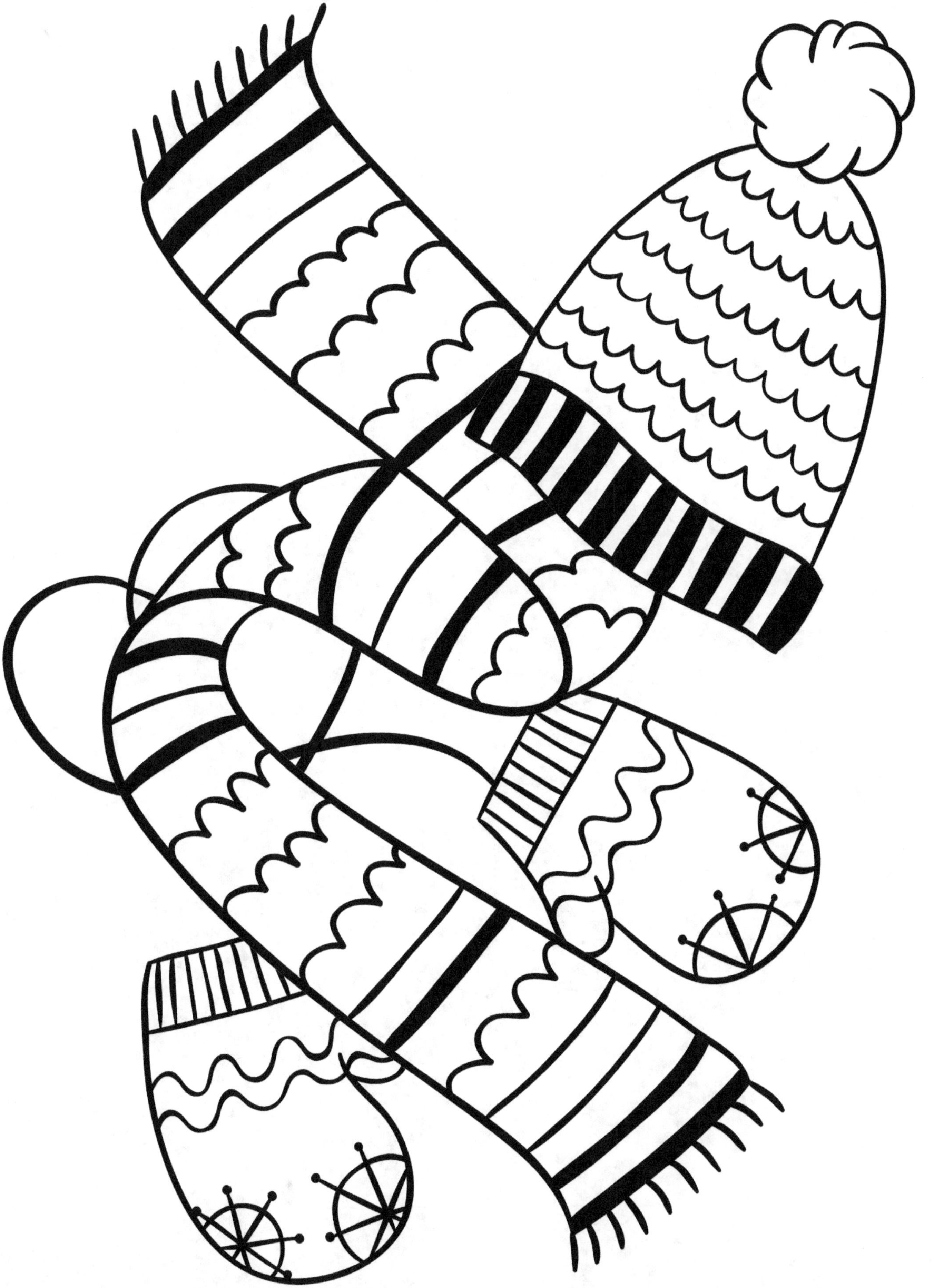

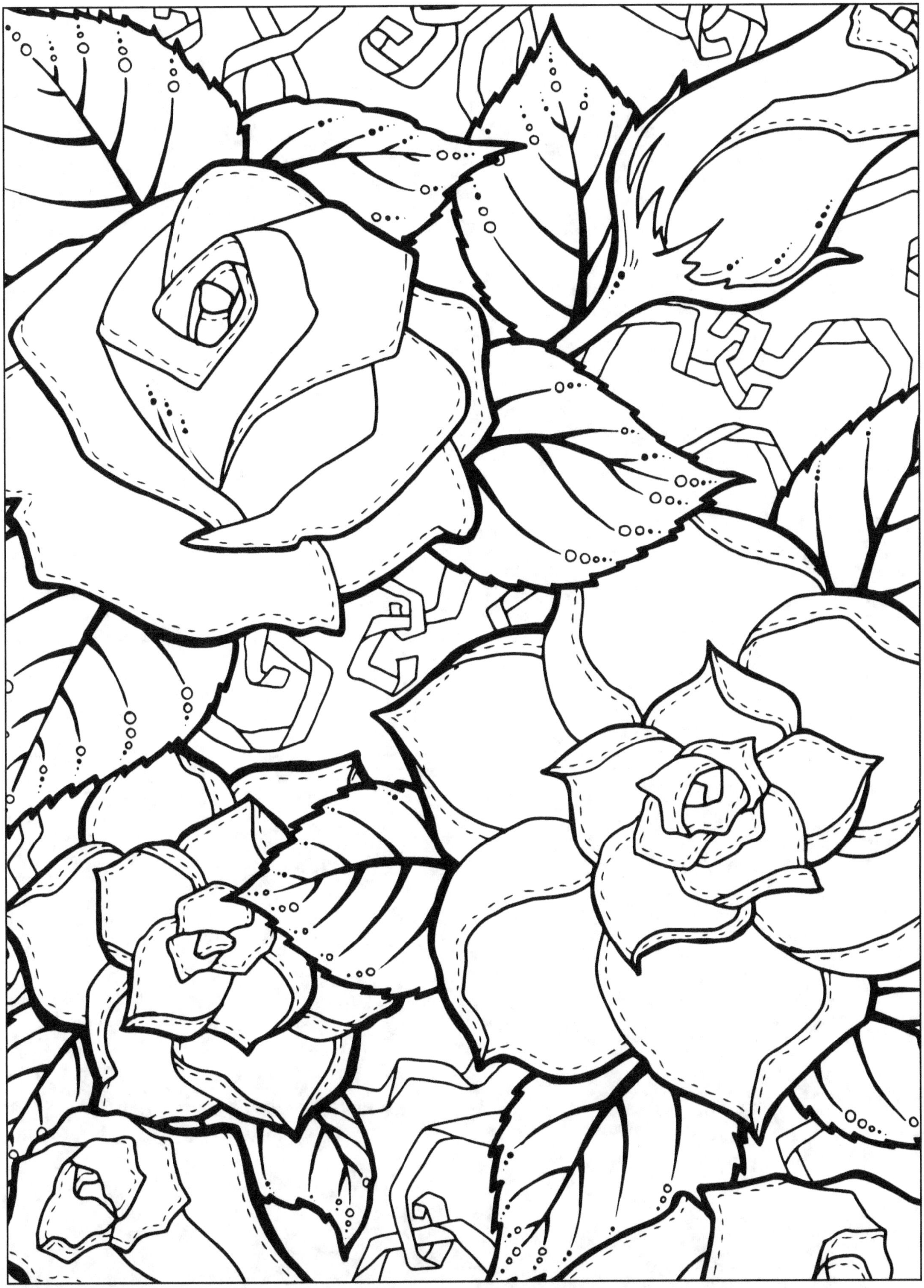

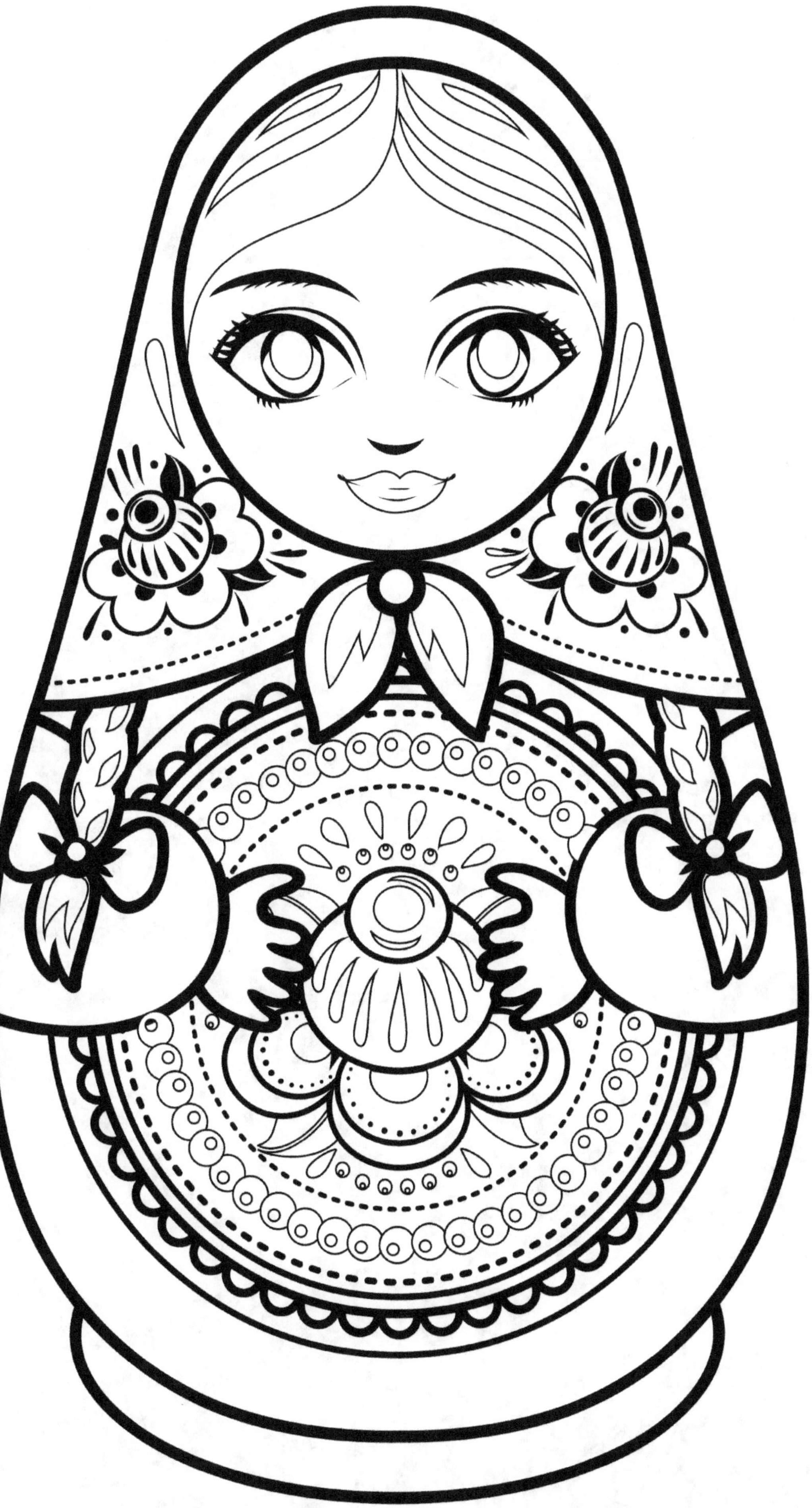

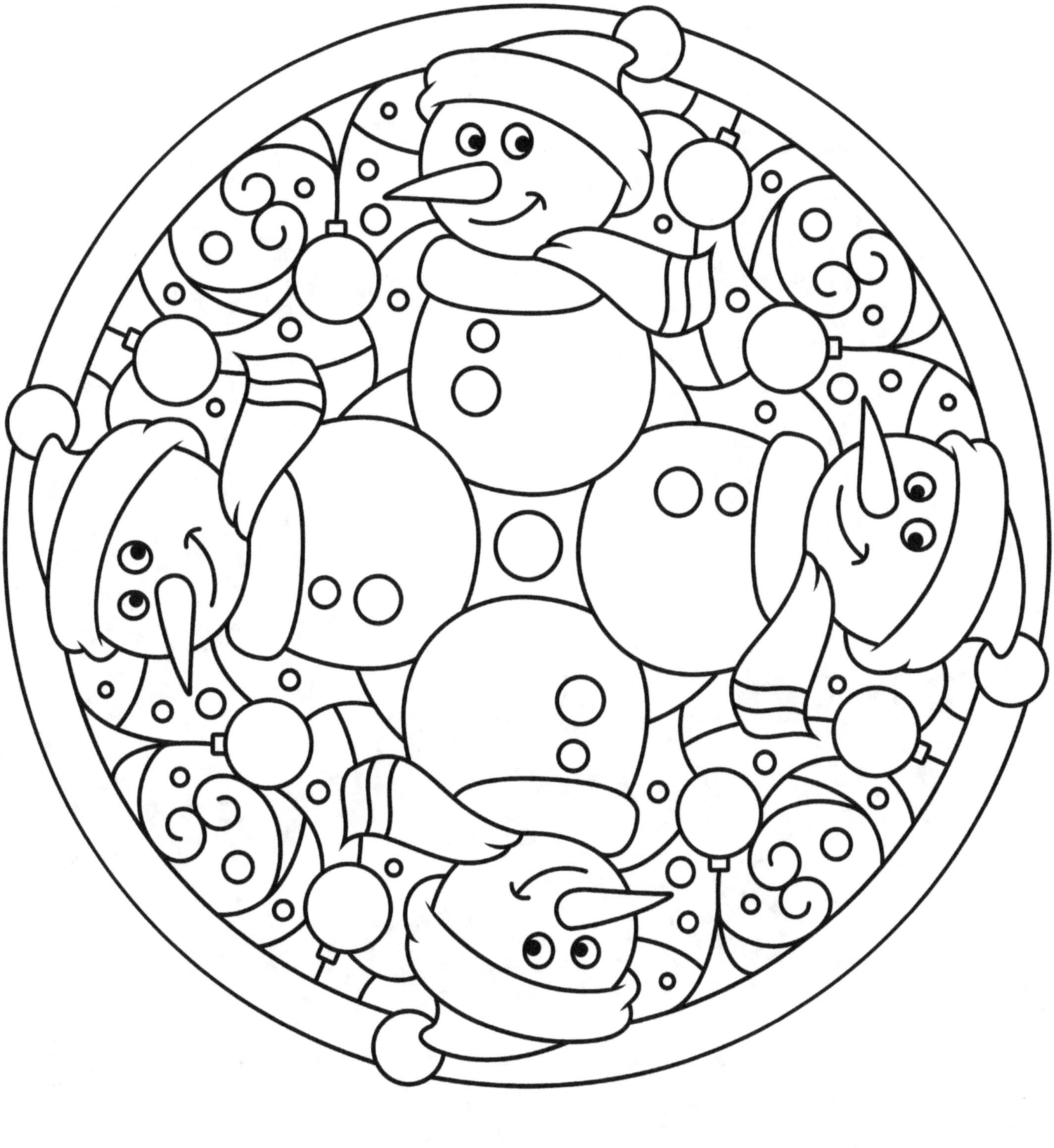

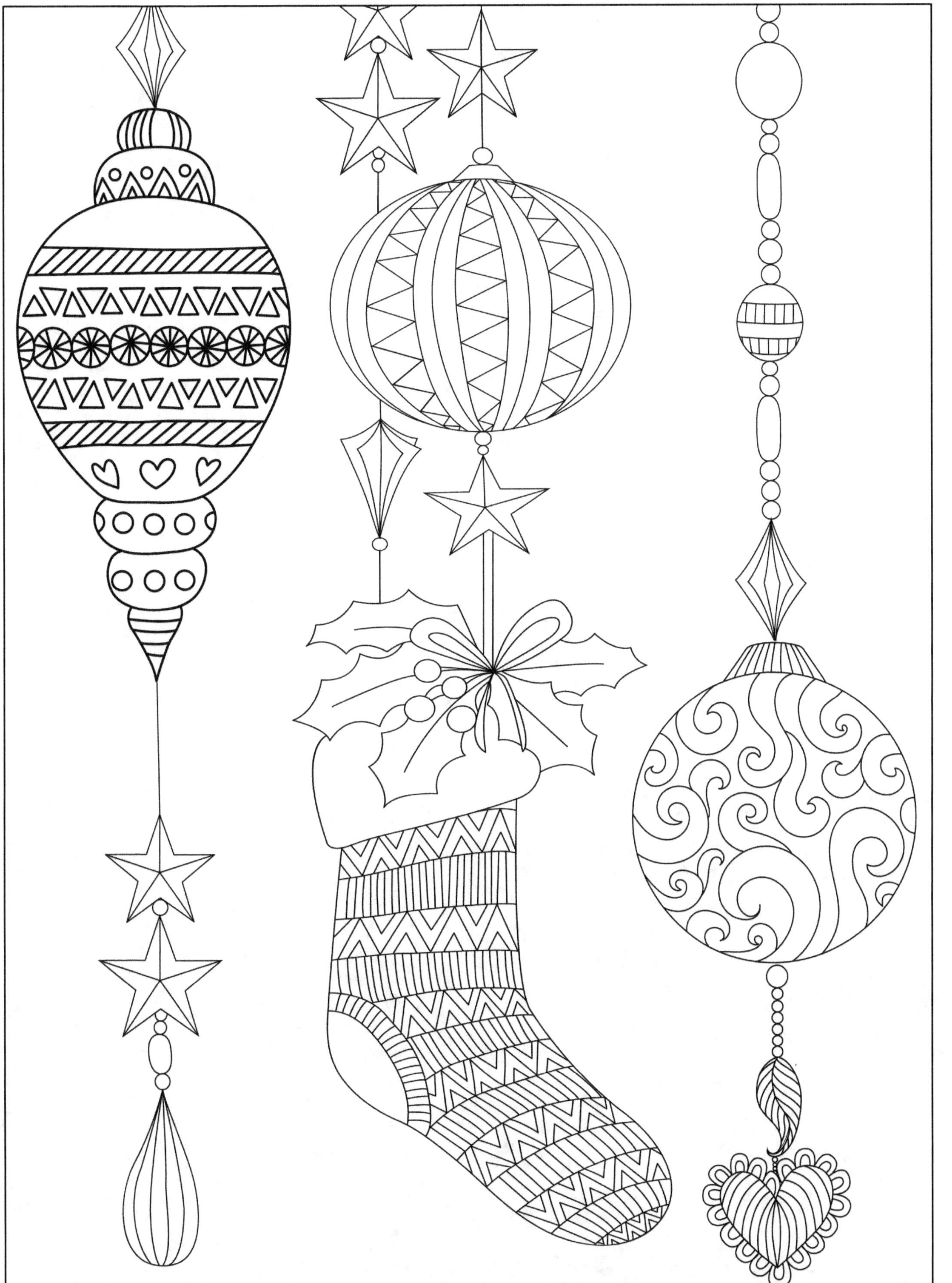

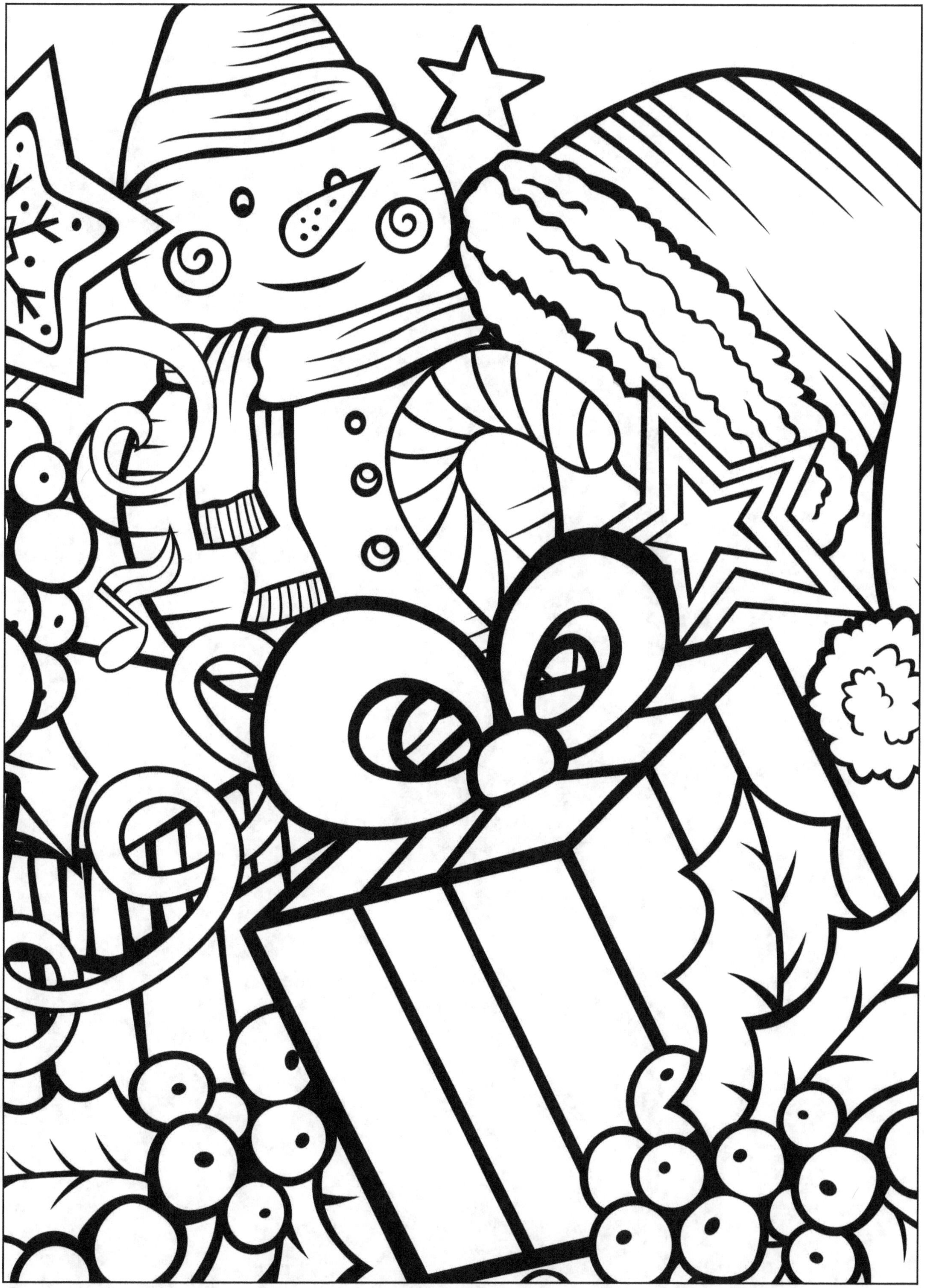

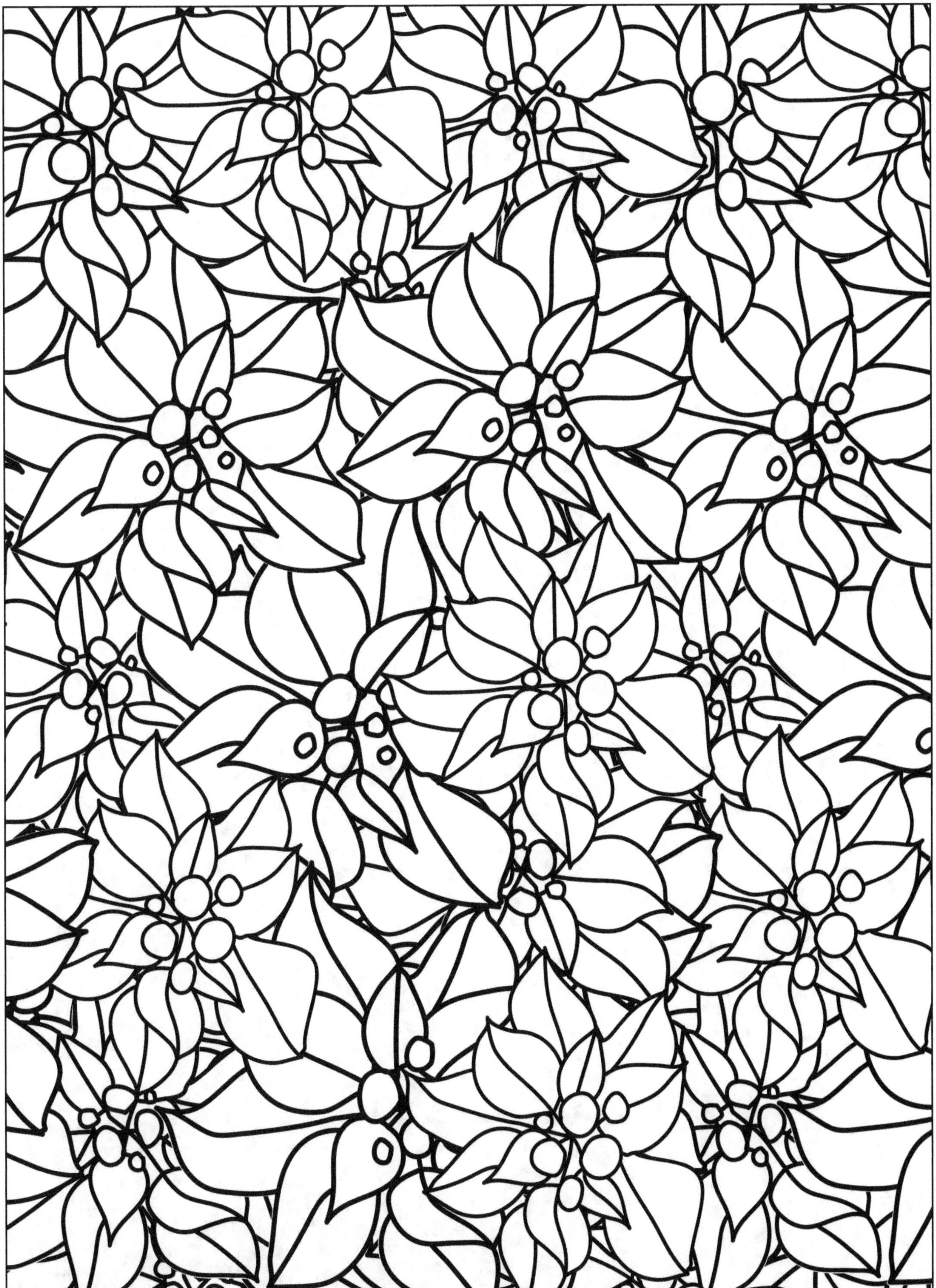

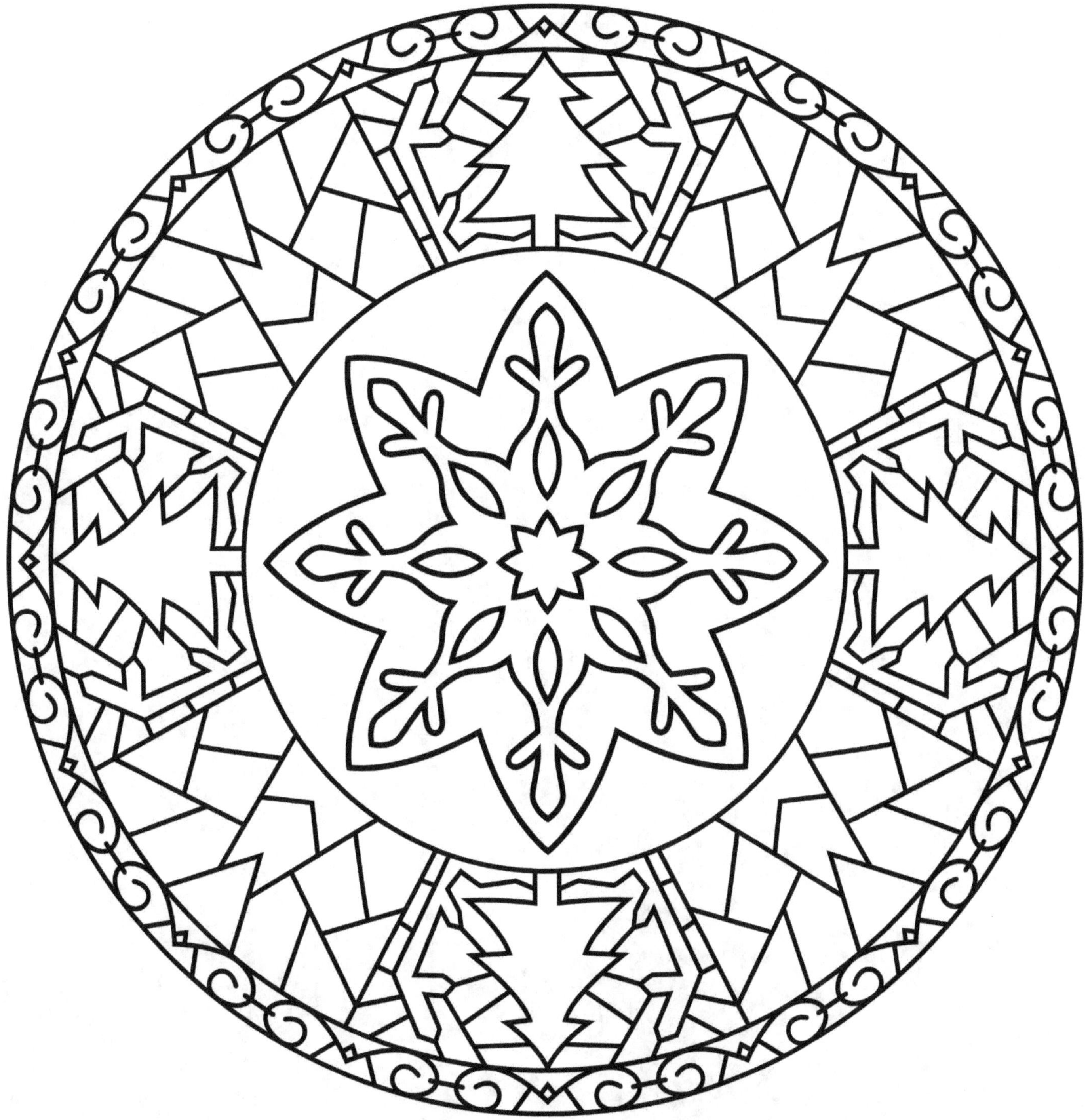

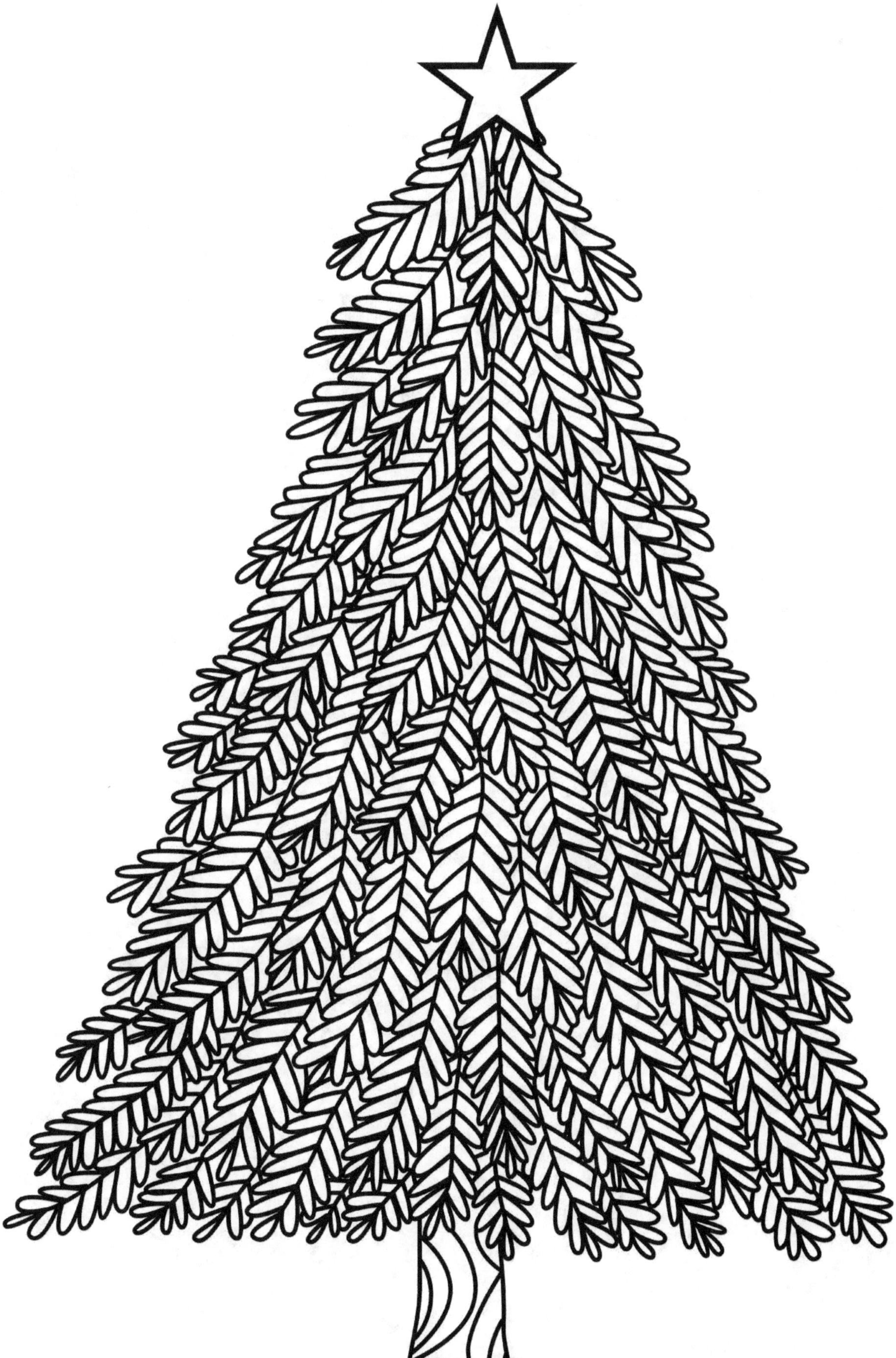

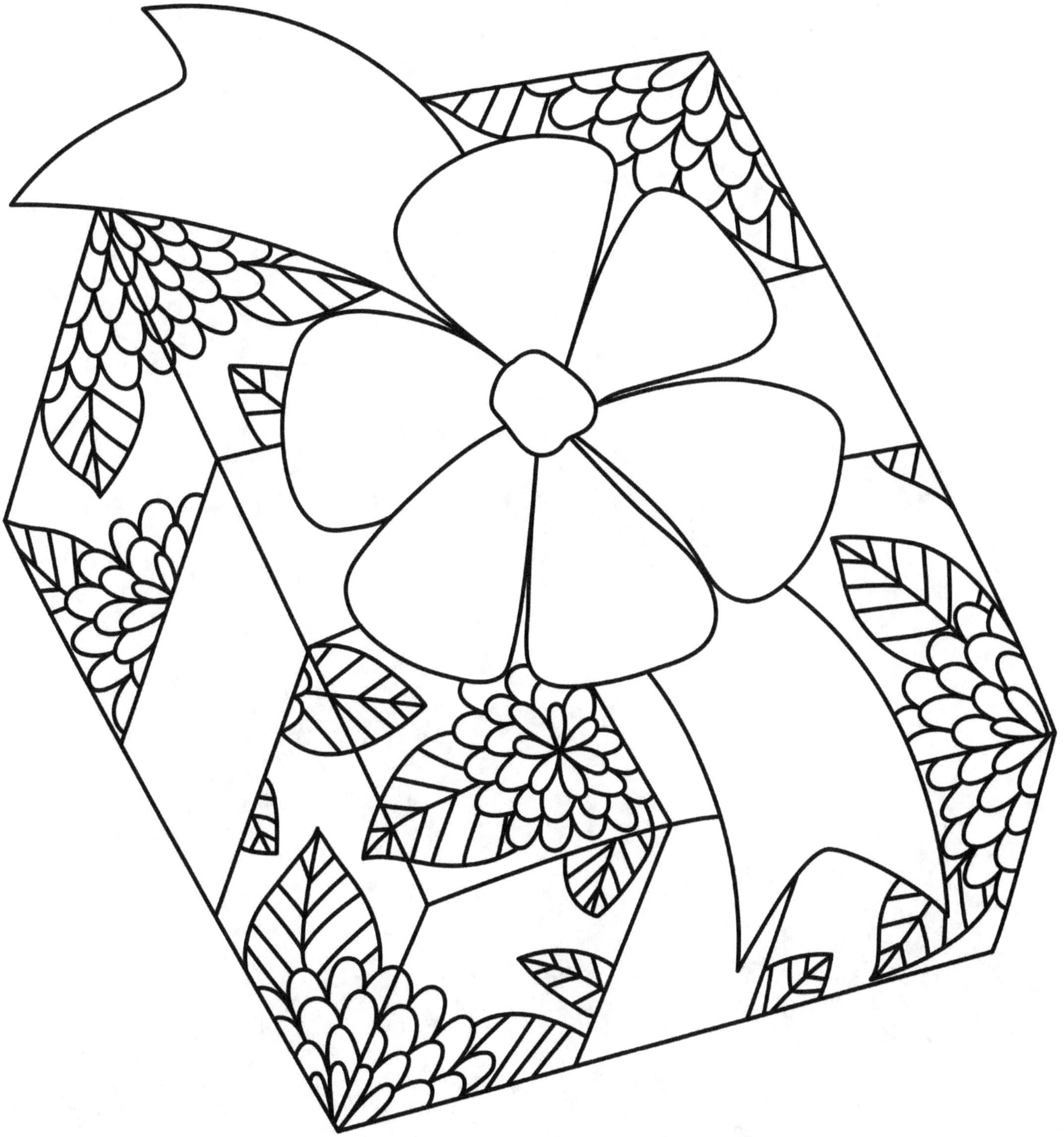

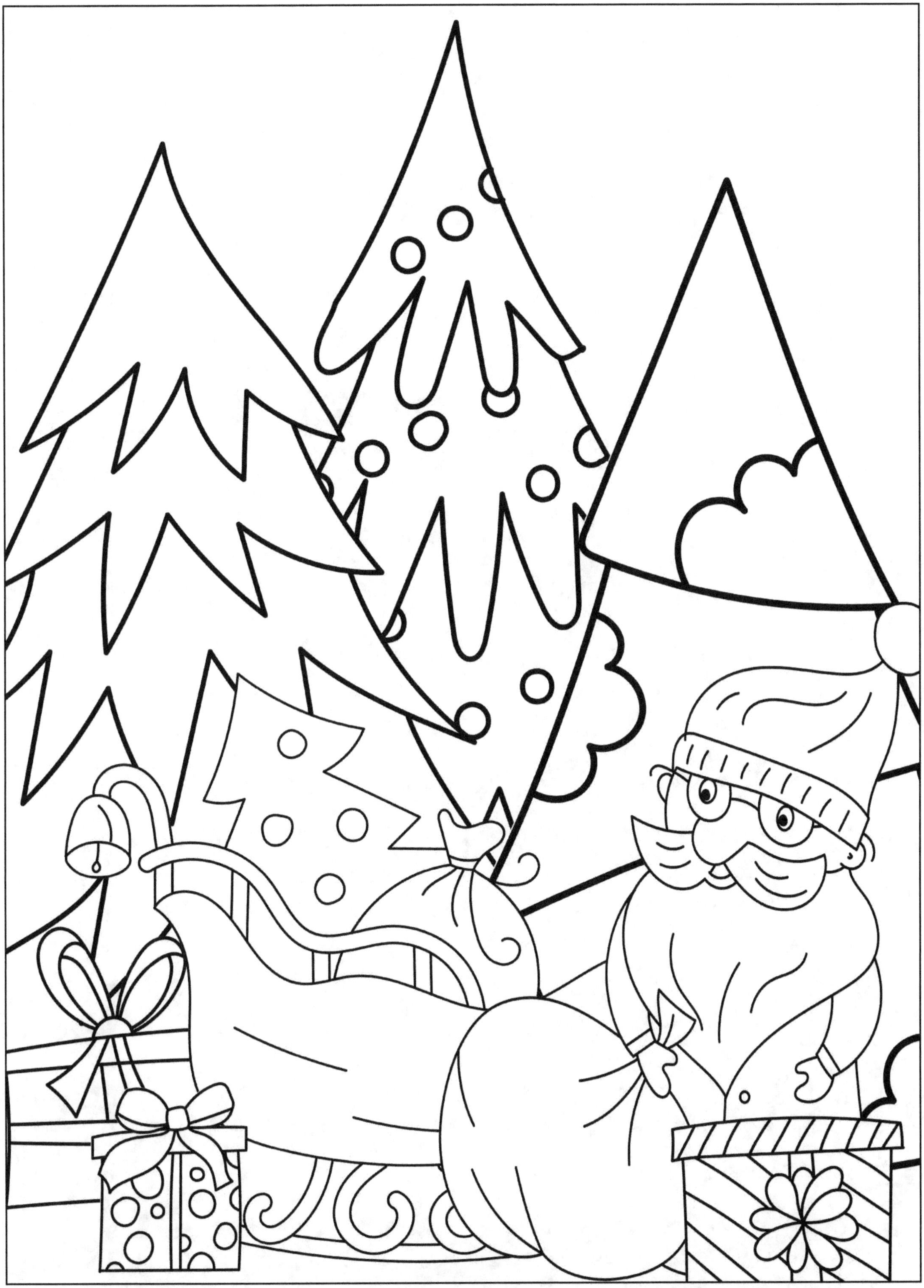

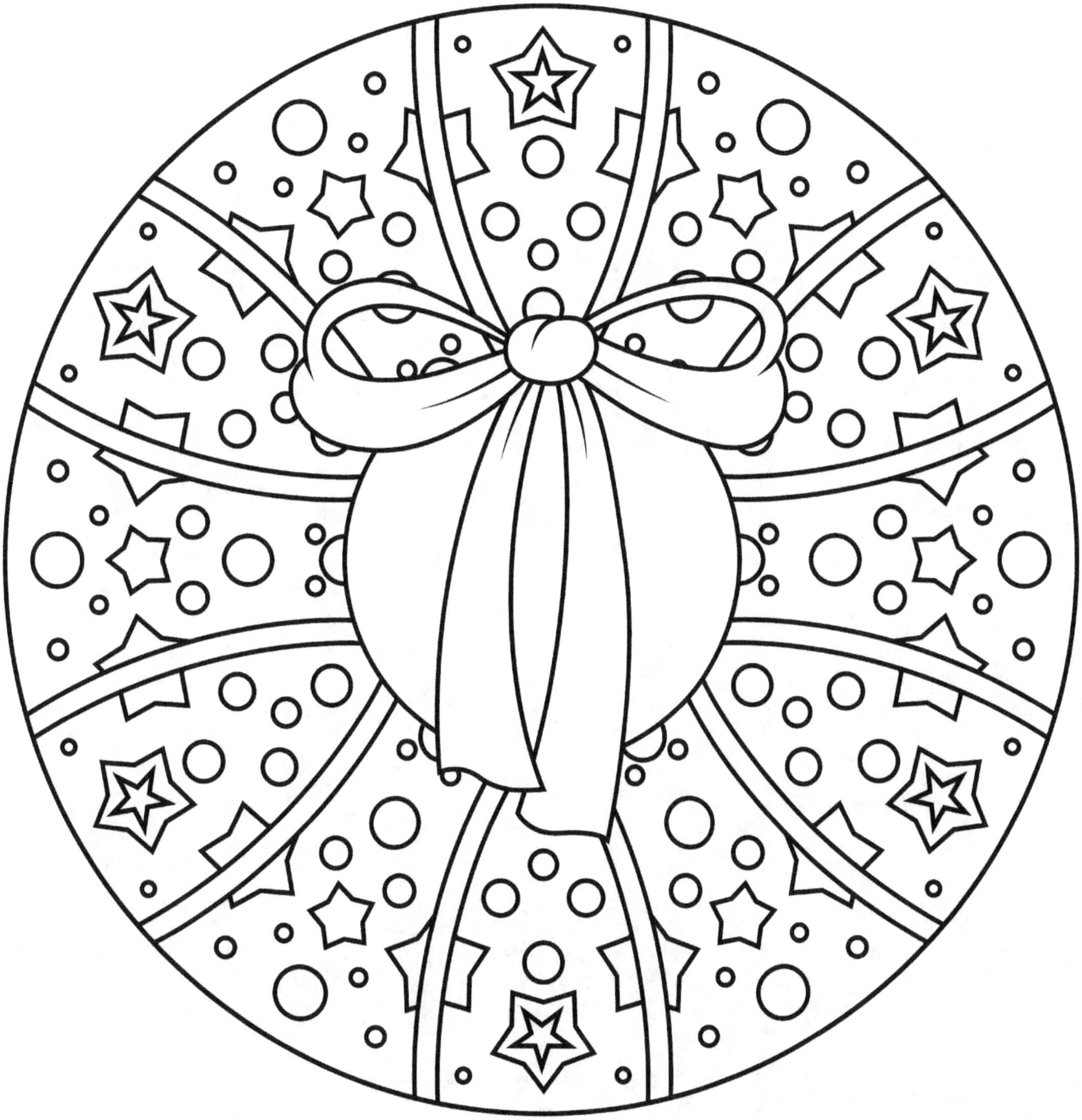

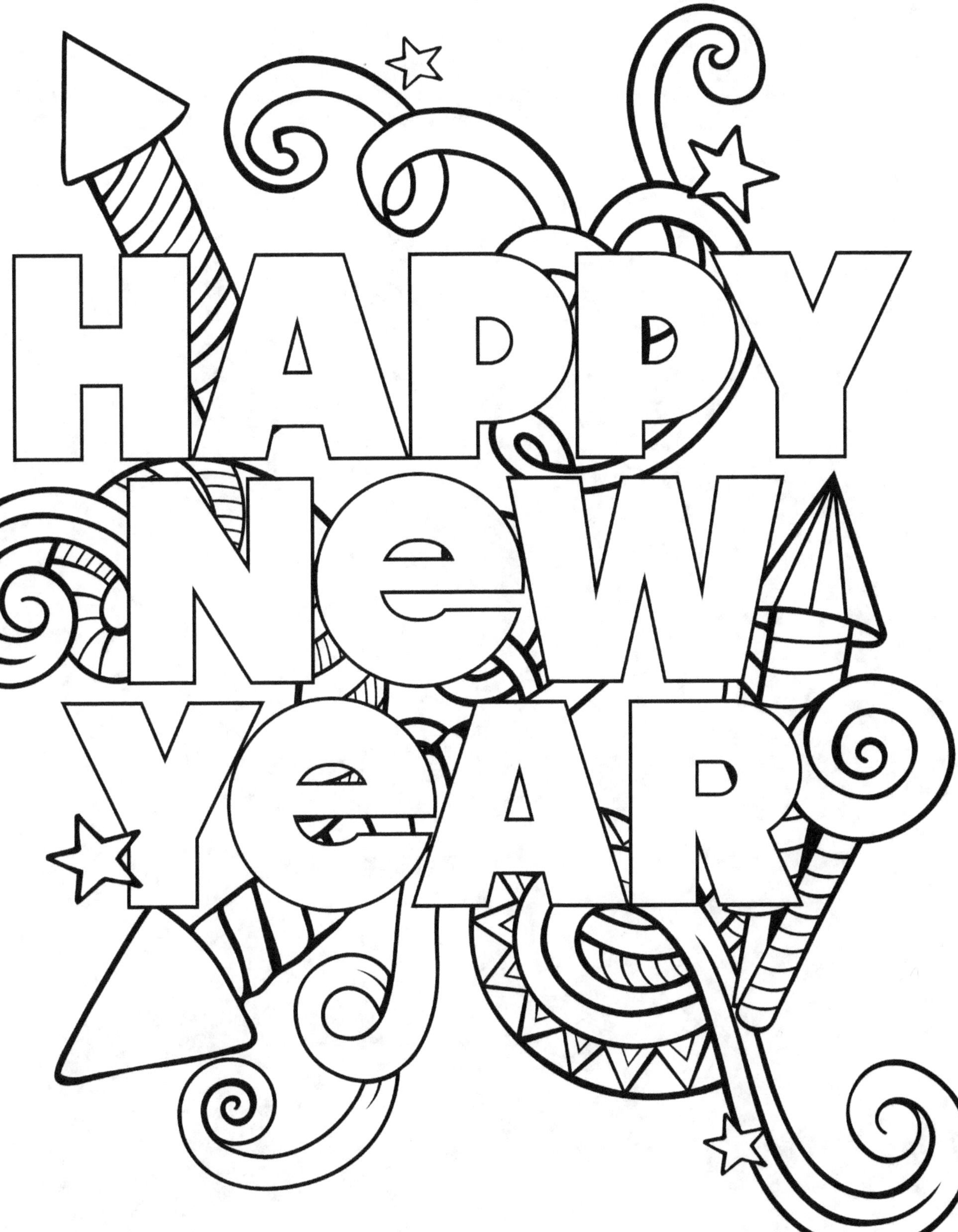
HAPPY
NEW
YEAR

TEST YOUR COLORS HERE.

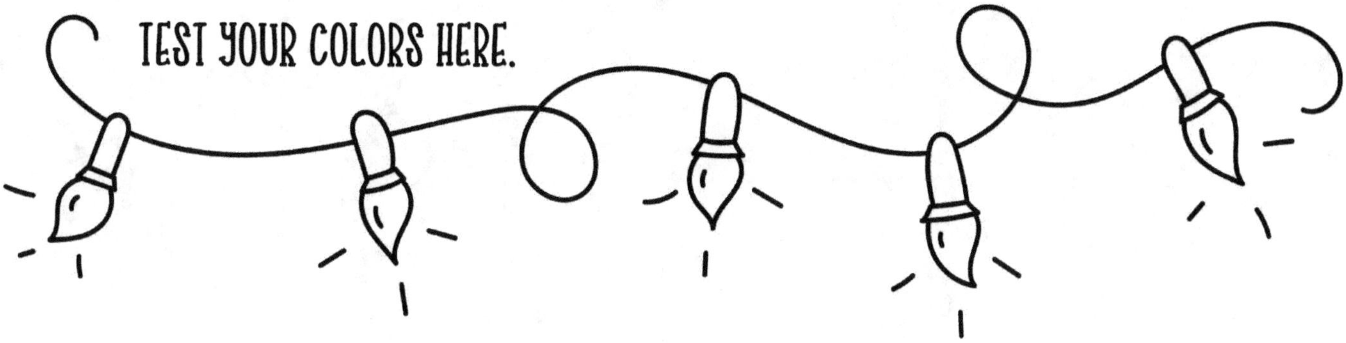

www.ingramcontent.com/pod-product-compliance
Lightning Source LLC
Chambersburg PA
CBHW081739220526
45468CB00008B/2165